COACHING

KIDS

TEEBALL

BY

Mike Daney

COACHING KIDS TEEBALL

First printing, April, 1985
American Youth Sports Publishing Company
24365 San Fernando Road   Suite 193
Newhall, California 91321

ISBN# 0-933715-00-5

DEDICATION

This book is dedicated to both my Dad and my son,
whose interactions, I believe, are significantly
enhanced by the common denominator called, "sports".

Thanks Dad for giving me a push into sports,
and thanks Mikie for responding so nicely to my push.

ACKNOWLEDGMENTS

The "physical fundamentals" in every sports book has parts that avail themselves to potential controversies. There are exceptions to every principle because the human body has an unlimited diversity of variables.

Nonetheless, **Mike Gillespie**, who is head coach at the College of the Canyons in Valencia, California, has an incredible repertoire of facts concerning these physical fundamentals, and I was fortunate to enlist him to analyze and critique the book from the standpoint of baseball fundamentals. Though a large part of his knowledge is too advanced for teeballers, the introductory foundation toward future sound fundamentals has been well established herein. Without his help and without knowing he was available to discuss specific principles, this book would not have achieved the credibility it now has.

Mike Gillespie played for Rod Dedeaux at U.S.C. in 1960, '61 and '62. During that time the Trojans were dominating the college baseball scene and won the 1961 NCAA National Championship, and were runners-up in 1960 and '62. Mike played an instrumental part as outfielder and second baseman in the success of those teams.

He began his coaching career at Rolling Hills High School where he coached from 1960 to 1970 winning 3 League Championships.

He has coached at College of the Canyons since 1971 winning 9 Conference Championships, and 2 California State Championships.

In 1981 and 1983 he was elected the National J. C. Co-Coach of the Year.

The front cover was designed by Marie Stephens.

The models for the 30 illustrations were Erik
Stephens and Mike Daney Jr. These ballplayers are
eleven years old and out of teeball but are blessed
with good form. Boys older than your teeballers can
provide a much more attractive model for your players
to emulate when shown examples of their form.

The coach pictured in a few of the illustrations is
yours truly.

Kris Gunn gave important impetus to the book through
her excellent transcribing of my original dictations.

A special thanks to my assistant coach, Sid Allen.
Sid was tremendously helpful in the task of
conducting the coaching chores. He was quick and
accurate in his evaluation of talent; and
beneficially philosophical about the importance and
perspective of what we were to accomplish. Having a
super assistant coach made it more fun and very
memorable.

CONTENTS

INTRODUCTION - THE KIDS

It has been my opinion for many years that a child's
involvement in sports is a good, wholesome, healthy
and educational thing to do. Most agree it intro-
duces a child to the "team" concept and therefore
provides a forum under which the child can share,
work, play, and compete in a group environment for
a common and obvious goal, to win.

But there are more important goals at this age level
than "to win". And the concept of "winning" which is
still under scrutiny for its potentiality in damaging
as well as enhancing ones self-esteem, with all the
ramifications and related effects that has, must be
dealt with by a coach if he is to conduct a training
philosophy that achieves that greatest amount of
benefit to the participants.

The determining factor between achieving a "win" or
suffering a "loss" is the comparative accumulation of
runs. This is an easy and obvious bench mark to use
in judging the success of a team, its players, a
coach, and a coaching philosophy.

But there may be more important struggles going on
during the life of a baseball team that are much more
difficult to monitor and evaluate. Nonetheless, a
coach cannot permit himself to overlook these other
struggles. And though the success of his effort in
these areas may be much more difficult to assess, if
he conceptualizes on them, if he gives them ample
time in his planning process, if he is aware of their

1

potential as well as detrimental effect on individuals, then he has taken a big step in achieving an approach to coaching kids that will promote the game to the benefit of all.

As a preface to the twelve chapters of rules, fundamentals, strategy, and organizational tips that follow this "Introduction" I present to you some thoughts by Dr. Arlene Sylvers, who is a noted child therapist, and school psychologist. Her work in our district has helped many children with difficult problems, and I think she is an excellent one to stimulate a new or even old coach into contemplating a possibly valid and insightful view of a group of people I call "kids".

TO COACHES, POTENTIAL COACHES AND PARENTS:

As you perceive your young Teeball player tentatively approach the tee for the first time, what fantasies are being conjured up in your mind? Does your fantasy project you into the future where you are observing your "own" offspring coming up to bat as the star hitter of a major league team? Perhaps, instead your fantasy is regressive and you see your youngster as the successful and popular ball player you secretly dreamed you would be.

If you also happen to be the parent coaching the team, is your primary goal to see that "these kids win", or do you view Teeball as a learning experience which could be great fun?

These are important questions to ask yourself because if you are projecting into the future or the past or trying to teach the team first and foremost to be competitive, you are doing your child and the team a disservice.

At this point you may say, "Hey wait a minute, what's wrong with competition?" or "Why shouldn't I push my kid to be all s/he could be?". I would then have to reply, that there is not a thing wrong with competition and that people should strive to be all they can. However, there is a time, developmentally, when the concept of competition can be understood and an earlier time when it's just confusing. We strive to be all we can, not when we are pushed beyond our readiness, but when we feel good about ourselves, when we enjoy the challenge, and are instrinsically motivated to pursue that which we strive for.

Let's look at what I mean when I say "developmentally". The age children start to play Teeball is generally five or six. That is a relatively brief period to have been alive. Although rapidly growing, a five year old has had only a short time to develop and experience the world. The information a child this age has had to assimilate is vast and I am often amazed at just how much five year olds learn in this short period of time.

Language has been developing since birth but only from around age two is your child communicating verbally. After only three or three and a half years of learning to communicate, a word such as "competition" is very strange; and, what does "winning" mean anyhow?

As a five year old wise beyond his years once told me with a shrug of his shoulders, "If I win, then I'm good and my dad likes me". "What does that mean?" I inquired. "I think it means I have to hit the ball."

For the first five years in a child's life the central and peripheral nervous systems are still developing. Mylenization of all the nerve fibers in the cerebral cortex of the brain have not yet taken place for perceptual development to be complete; spatial relationships, perceptual skills, and muscle groups are still developing.

Psychologically, at age five children are just learning to be independent of their parents and can tolerate separation for longer periods of time than previously experienced. However, they are still totally dependent on their parents' approval and possess a strong desire to please them. Parents are the most important source of their child's feeling of self-esteem. Parenting is one great responsibility!

Five year old children are just learning to be social beings and instead of the toddler's parallel play, they are learning to interact and play with each other. There is no doubt that whatever form it takes, play is the work of children. Through play children learn social rules, experience the opportunity to be creative and imaginative, and develop a sense of competency.

Though somewhat anxiously approaching the tee for the first time, can s/he be perceptually accurate? Sometimes. When s/he is not, do we get aggressive and push harder or do we choose to communicate how pleased we are that s/he tried so well?

I hope you would make the latter choice for that is the one which encourages willingness to try again while the former encourages defeat, i.e., "I can't do anything right; I might as well not try." Or worse,"...not play".

Maybe one of those children out on the field will become a baseball star or play baseball in high school or college, but right now s/he needs to learn about teamwork and how to be part of a team before even grasping the meaning of competition.

At this point you may be questioning your decision to have your child participate in a team sport but I must share with you that you are doing something important for your child!

Parents who involve their youngsters in Teeball or any team sport are providing them with a wonderful opportunity! It is an opportunity to develop spatial and perceptual skills which they cannot achieve in front of a television or with close paper and pencil work.

Sports enable children to learn social rules such as fairness and sportsmanship; to value teamwork so that when their team wins, even though they missed hitting or fielding a ball, they can feel a sense of pride. Mainly, they are learning how to have lots of fun with children their own age and with adults who care enough to see that they enjoy themselves, feel a sense of positive self-esteem, and help to develop a sense of competency whether they win or lose.

I personally admire and respect parents who provide such opportunities for their children for they are, indeed, enriching their lives.

Arlene Sylvers, Ph.D   School Psychologist
Marriage, Family and Child Therapist

Teeball is a game of sports that has enormous potential for providing enjoyable, exciting, and rewarding
experiences for coaches, players, and parents if it
is accepted for what-it-is. And what-it-is is a game
similar to baseball but with important differences.

Teeball is most commonly played by children from five
to ten years old who have unlimited potential matched
only by innumerable limitations. On the average
these children love to play and will surprise you at
their progress; but on the other hand they have a
short span of attention; may not consciously know
whether they want to play the game or not; lack
coordination, muscular dexterity and stamina; and
most importantly may not have any concept or appreciation for competition.

Fortunately, the rules of teeball take into consideration these player potentials and limitations but by
their nature establish important differences from
ones normal perception of "baseball".

As a start, therefore, let's look at the basic differences in the rules of teeball from ordinary baseball
to give you your first insight into a sport the
Dodgers and Yankees never played.

IMPORTANT DIFFERENCES IN THE RULES
FROM REGULAR BASEBALL

1. The pitcher in Teeball, located in the same
    general area of the diamond as a pitcher in
    regular baseball, does not pitch. Instead,
    the ball is placed at home plate on a large
    tee from which it is batted.

    The tee usually stands about 3 feet high
    with a cone shaped receptacle on top that
    holds the ball. A rubber shaft extends
    down from the cone to a rubber base
    frequently shaped like home plate.

2. The teeball used is slightly different from
    your regulation baseball. It is the same
    size but it is covered with a rubber coat-
    ing and contains a large cork center which
    makes it weigh less than a regulation base-
    ball. The lighter weight is considerably
    better for the children because it seems
    less dangerous to them (and it is).

    The surface of the ball is about as hard as
    a regulation baseball, however in some
    playgrounds in recent years a softer,
    spongier type baseball not uncharacteristic
    of a "nerf ball" has been used and inter-
    changed with the normal teeball. In
    addition there is the "IncrediBall" made
    of a solid polyurethane core (light weight)
    and nylon cover which is gaining in teeball
    acceptance and is a practical advancement
    in teeball equipment.

3. There are no bench warmers in teeball. All
    team members play at all times during a
    teeball game.

    This means that if you have 12 players show
    for the game, you use all 12 players simul-
    taneously on defense, and all 12 must
    appear sequentially in the batting rotation.
    (If you thought it might be difficult
    coaching nine mature players in the field

6

who are attentive to the game, try coaching twelve immature ones who are not.)

This rule, however, is a blessing in disguise to the players, coaches and parents. It can't be done in basketball and flag football because those games would get out of control with so many players on the court or field at the same time, but it is done in teeball, and done, I might add, successfully. All the players feel good about themselves because they're all playing all the time; the coaches don't have to make that difficult decision of who's to sit on the bench; and the parents are all able to see their children play the entire game.

4. The counting of outs is not pertinent in determining the end of an inning. All the players on a team will bat to complete an offensive inning.

   Therefore, outs only serve to reduce base runners who could potentially score in that inning.

5. Each play is concluded and the ball is dead when the batted ball is in the control of the pitcher while he is positioned within the "pitching circle". This circle of approximately 10 feet in diameter surrounds the pitching rubber.

   In order to end an inning with runners on base the ball, batted by the last batter, must be returned to the pitcher within the pitching circle.

   This is a key segment of the rules and it gives recognition to the fact that the defensive abilities of the children are considerably underdeveloped.

6. The allowed advancement of a base runner in respect to the pitching circle rule (item 5 above) is determined by the base runner's position in relationship to a chalk marker

placed half-way between each base,
including one between third base and home
plate.

If a base runner advances past the half-way
marker before the pitcher has control of
the ball in the pitching circle, he is
awarded the advanced base.

This rule causes the most difficulty for an
umpire because most games are only refereed
by one "ump", and the game situation may
require him to measure the advancement of
three base runners while simultaneously
observing when the ball is in the control
of the pitcher while in the pitching circle.
This would be a formidable task for a
skilled professional umpire let alone a
playgrounds amateur.

7.   There is no stealing, and there is no
     leading off the base until the ball has
     been batted from the tee.

8.   A combination of three missed swings or
     foul balls constitutes a strike-out.

     Believe it or not, young batters occasion-
     ally miss the ball which is sitting
     indefensively on the tee.

9.   The normal teeball game is designed to go
     approximately four teeball innings, or an
     hour and 15 minutes to an hour and a half.

     But remember a teeball inning is much longer
     than a regulation baseball inning because a
     team bats its entire lineup every inning.
     Thus, if you have twelve players show for
     the game, your team will get 48 "at bats"
     in the four innings.

10. Two coaches are permitted within the field
     of play when their team is on defense.

     This gives the coaches a better opportunity
     to control the positioning of their defensive

players and influence their activity.

Some cynical observers believe the rule was
designed to help the coach warn a fielder
when the ball was coming at him so the
fielder could get out of its way.

11.   Batting helmets are mandatory in most
        leagues. They should be called "base
        running helmets" in teeball because not too
        many players get hit in the head while
        batting from a tee.

It is always good practice for the coach to be
familiar with the rules of the sport he is about to
coach. In this case the coach must become familiar
with the rules of baseball and teeball. Some
situations will occur in your games that you never
saw watching Monday Night Baseball.

Young umpires are sometimes easily intimidated by a
more mature coach, and your opposing coach just may
influence him on a controversial call relating to
rules you're not familiar with.

Here's some situations you may want to check
the local rules on:

o   Two runners end up on one base with the
        pitcher in control of the ball in the
        pitching circle.

        Is any runner automatically out even though
        he has not been tagged? Does one runner
        have to return to a base? Which one?
        Could they both be out?

o   The pitcher, in control of the ball, runs
        through the pitching circle to tag a runner
        out between first and second.

        What happened when the pitcher ran with the
        ball through the pitching circle? Does the
        tag still count?

o   The pitcher covers home plate on a play,
        and the shortstop holds the ball within the

pitching circle.

The opposing coach feels the play has not ended and his base runners can continue advancing. Is this true?

o   The batter throws his bat accidentally while swinging.

Does he get a warning, or is he out?

o   With the bases loaded, the last batter is thrown out at first base.

Is the inning over?

o   A batter hits a ground ball back to the pitcher who gains control within the circle.

Is the batter out? Can a runner on first advance to second even though he didn't reach the halfway marker by the time the pitcher had control of the ball within the circle?

In implementing the rules of teeball remember they are designed to protect the children both physically and psychologically. The rules are designed to recognize the related limitations of the children both physically and emotionally. If the coach also recognizes these limitations early in his introduction to the game (without allowing them to inhibit the potentiality of his coaching), he will easily grasp the significance of the resultant strategies he must use in his attempt to win and will be more readily and justifiably content with their outcome.

OTHER BASIC DIFFERENCES FROM REGULAR BASEBALL

The differences in the rules from regular baseball have much to do with making the game quite different from regular baseball. The physical abilities of the players, and the desire to somewhat reduce the full competitive impact of advanced baseball cause other

differences. Here's some you should be aware of in
order to start out with a comfortable feel about the
game.

- o   Catching the ball during the first two
        years of teeball (flyweight level) is an
        infrequent event. Therefore, many throwing
        plays to the bases or back to the pitcher
        are made by <u>rolling</u> the ball. Some have
        argued that this is an expedient way of
        coaching the game which produces victories
        but doesn't advance the child's develop-
        ment. I don't agree with this observation.

- o   Catching the ball in the next two years of
        teeball (mightymite level) is a much more
        frequent occurrence. Normally a coach can
        find two, three or four players on the team
        that have the coordination, and courage to
        catch the ball frequently. These are the
        players the coach assigns to his strategic
        "out positions".

- o   You will find the entire contingent of your
        twelve-man defensive team residing some-
        where within the confines of a softball
        infield. The geographical position of a
        normal outfielder will be toward the edge
        of the infield where it meets the grass
        of the outfield. This is obviously due to
        the overall lack of hitting power of the
        batters.

- o   Usually there is no player assigned to the
        position of catcher. This is done because
        there is no pitch; there is very infre-
        quent need to make a play at the plate;
        and as a precautionary step to eliminate
        the possibility of a child getting hit by a
        bat.

- o   The "one size fits all" baseball cap for
        adults is not an appropriate type of cap
        for small children. There is a child's
        adjustable cap whose crown is not as bulky
        as the adult cap. It is one that will stay
        on their heads better while they play, and
        it looks a lot smarter.

11

LEAGUE PLAY

There seems to be little distinction between league play in teeball and any other type of baseball.

A ten game regular season with the potential for two or three post season tournament games seems adequate and not overbearing.

The categorization of age groups is somewhat flexible, but it is unwise to place children competing against each other whose age difference is greater than two years.

One local Parks Department designated 5 and 6 year olds for the "flyweight" division, and 7 and 8 year olds for the "mightymite' division. The 9 and 10 year olds advanced to softball even though teeball, with its stationary hitting target, may have had its advantages.

The two year groupings were determined by a specific cutoff date. One method easy to verify and manage is a grouping by calendar year of birth. This method has the disadvantage of forcing some children who were born late in the year, and who may be competing in other sports like flag football, soccer, and basketball, to always be the youngest in competition at whatever sport happens to be in season.

A better method is to have the cutoff date be the first of the month beginning the selection of the teams and start of practice. Under this method, for example, if Randy was born in December, he may be one of the younger boys for basketball starting in January, but he will be one of the older ones for football which ends in December.

USE THIS SPACE FOR YOUR NOTES

Now that you are familiar with the rules and some of
the basic differences between teeball and regular
baseball, I am going to take you on a trip around the
infield and outfield in a discussion about specific
defensive positions.

We'll need to cover the talent requirements for each
position and how that position should be played at
this level of competition.

Don't feel at a disadvantage if you don't have a good
working knowledge of the general requirements of each
position. If you do, the concepts I teach will just
come a lot quicker. If you don't, then the material
is here for you to learn.

The Pitcher

The most significant feature of the pitcher is
that he does not pitch. The pitcher must stand
in the pitching circle until the ball is batted
from the tee and then make the best defensive
move in retrieving the batted ball, or control-
ling a ball thrown from the other fielders into
the circle to end the inning. He may also be
called upon to race home after fielding a ground
ball, to force out or tag a runner coming down
the line from third base.

The pitcher should have the best defensive abilities on the team. He is involved in every play whether initiating an out at a base, or ending play in the pitching circle. He should have the ability to field a high percentage of ground balls and have superior fielding range when compared to the other players.

It is important that the pitcher have a fairly good understanding of the rules of the game, or at least have the instinct for the right thing to do. He is the key person influencing the activity of the infield.

A good fielding pitcher can make a poor defensive team look good, or a poor fielding pitcher can make a pretty good fielding team look bad. He can give the rest of the fielders confidence; he can "show them the way"; he can intimidate the base runners, and keep the opponent's running game restricted. He is the player the coaches "key-off-of" in directing the aggressiveness of defensive play. He is the backbone, cornerstone and foundation of the defense, and he hasn't even started to pitch the ball yet.

Since most of the batters will not have the strength nor ability to hit the ball very far, the pitcher should have the ability, and be taught to charge slowly hit ground balls. He will have many opportunities to throw runners out at first base, or other bases on force plays on balls that were tapped very slowly in front of him. He must be coached to charge the ball, pick it up with confidence, and in a timely but not hurried manner, throw or roll the teeball to the baseman for the out.

The Catcher

As briefly mentioned before, the catcher's position usually doesn't exist in teeball. There are three principal reasons for this:

1. There is no pitch to the plate requiring the catcher to receive the ball. The ball batted off of the tee is usually propelled in a direction away from the normal catcher's position.

15

2.   Teeball rules require all players in the
      catchers position to wear catching equip-
      ment including a face guard or mask, chest
      protector and shin guards. Equipment like
      this would be very restrictive for these
      little guys and handicap them considerably
      in their ability to perform.

3.   Lastly, the catcher is in a position where
      he can easily get hit with a thrown bat, or
      get in the way of a batter swinging the
      bat in warming up, or striking at the ball.

There are a few situations, however, usually at
the mightymite level where there is a need to
station a defensive player near the plate close
to the catchers position. An example of this is
when the defensive team absolutely cannot allow
another run to cross the plate, and the defensive play has to be to the plate. If this were
the case, then the coach may want to position
some player close to home plate to receive a
possible throw from one of the infielders.

The First Baseman

First base is a key "out position". The first
baseman has more opportunities to make outs for
his team than any other position on the field.
No matter how good the coach's defensive
strategy is, and no matter how good the other
fielders field the ball and throw or roll it to
first base, if the first baseman can't catch the
ball, no out will be recorded, and all the
practice, strategy and effort will have been in
vain.

Your second best fielder in the category of
"catching" therefore should be your first baseman. He needn't have an accurate or strong
throwing arm, but he should have a relatively
good fielding range. Most of his throwing
plays, however, will be directed back to the
pitcher, and the chance of him doing this
inaccurately can be reduced by having him run
the ball most of the way back to the pitcher,
ending it with a short underhand toss.

His requirements are not too unlike requirements of any first baseman in regular baseball. It is not, however, an advantage for him to be left-handed.

He must be eager to learn how to field ground balls and have a higher level of courage than most of the other players. Few throws will come in his direction that are perfectly launched, thus it would be helpful if he were the type that liked the challenge of stopping balls frequently misdirected.

The Rightside Shortstop

This position doesn't exist in normal baseball. It is a shortstop stationed between the first baseman, and the second baseman to plug the hole into right field.

The limited range of your infielders allows this new position to be created. For example; if you have 60 feet between first and second base, and the first and second basemen each can cover three feet to their right or left, that leaves 48 feet for a batter to hit to. So we reduce the odds for the batter by inventing the rightside shortstop.

He should play this position equidistant between the first and second basemen. He should have some of the same abilities that a shortstop has except he doesn't need a good arm. Almost all of his throws will be to the first baseman who will only be 10 to 30 feet away. Long-range throws won't be necessary, but underhand tosses should be common.

Most batters will be right-handed, therefore balls hit to his side of the infield will not be hit with the same power or crispness as balls hit to the other side of the infield.

He should be the type of player who is trainable in the function of backing-up first base. Many poor throws to first will give him a lot of opportunities to make an important contribution to the defensive play. He will be aided in his backup function, of course, by the right

fielder, but as you will learn about later, the
right fielder is not exactly the player you will
want to rely on frequently.

The Second Baseman

The second baseman is another "out" position,
however, because he fields behind the pitcher
who is usually one of the best fielders on the
team and because, in general, there are usually
fewer plays at second base, his opportunities
for making outs will be few. The pitcher's
normal play after fielding the ball will be to
throw to first base. A throw to second is
usually a longer throw and frequently made to a
moving target since coverage will come from the
second baseman or shortstop who will not normally play on top the bag.

The second baseman should be a good enough
fielder to give the team a chance to make outs
at second if the force strategy provides for it.
And there will be opportunities for force outs
especially when slow base runners at first must
go to second on a ball hit to the left side.

In addition, he should be good enough to assist
with the throws coming in from the outfield, and
getting the ball back to the pitcher.

He can have just an average arm. Most throws
he'll make will be short, and if you haven't
guessed by now, he won't have to make the double
play throw going away from first base after
receiving a toss from the shortstop.

Though there are occasions when the second baseman can be very active, because of his distance
from the batters, and protection behind the
pitcher, he will probably be the infielder with
the least amount of activity.

The Shortstop

As with advanced baseball, the shortstop is a
very important position in teeball. Since most
batters are right-handed, their power and

ability to hit the ball to the left side of the infield seems common. The shortstop will have many more opportunities than most of the other infielders.

The shortstop should have a good arm. This requirement may be contingent upon the ability of the first baseman to catch, because if he can't, long throws to first by the shortstop won't be required.

He must make decisions with the coaches help as to tagging runners between second and third, or covering a base (second or third), or deciding to get the ball back to the pitcher. The short-stop can be looked upon as the second team leader in the infield. He should be fairly aggressive in getting involved in the play by calling for the ball from the outfield, or backing-up the pitcher, or backing-up throws to other bases.

Since children typically have fear of getting hit by a bad bounce off a ground ball, the shortstop will probably have to be one of your players with the least amount of fear of the ball.

Even as the first practices start the children with the least amount of fear will progress more rapidly than the others. You should consider this factor early in your selection of positions, for it will always be important to anticipate each child's progress in assigning him his responsibility, and his progress and natural ability can be greatly restricted by his fear of the ball. Since the shortstop will be the target of most of the hard hit ground balls, this courage factor should be considered seriously.

The Third Baseman

The third baseman is the second most important "out position" on the field. His out producing activity will center around force-outs at third base, and tagging runners coming in from second base.

And do not underestimate the potential for force

outs at third either. Remember, with 10 or 12 batters coming to the plate every inning in conjunction with the out production being as difficult as it is, you can rest assured that many runners will advance to third availing themselves to the force.

Like the shortstop, he will be the target of harder hit ground balls, therefore he should be a player with relatively little fear of the ball. It would be a real plus if he has a strong, accurate throwing arm, but again the need for this is very dependent upon the catching ability of the first baseman. In flyweight teeball, the need is minor, but in mightymite ball, with the first baseman's ability tremendously improved, the need is much higher.

The Outfield

In teeball the outfielders are usually your most inexperienced players. Because of the infrequency of fly balls hit to the outfield, and because of the inability of children to catch fly balls, the outfield is not usually an "out position".

The outfield is a good place to assign a player who really is not mature enough to play the infield. This is the player whose concentration level is worse than most (and unfortunately the inactivity of the outfield doesn't help that problem), who may be afraid of the ball to the point of rendering him ineffective in the infield, or who may be substantially undeveloped in his physical abilities.

The coach and players should not look at an outfield assignment as degrading or a form of "punishment". Many children who do not have the skills to play infield are better off in the outfield because they are not put into a position where they can embarrass themselves on every play. The humiliation of playing a strategic position and failing before your peers and parents is much more potentially destructive than playing a somewhat non-active position and becoming somewhat bored.

When activity does occur in the outfield, it usually is very critical. A ball hit into the outfield usually has "many runs" potential. Thus this aspect of the importance of the position can be emphasized to the team so that the assignment to the outfield is not demeaning.

In looking to place your three to five outfielders in the position that best contributes to your teams defensive performance, keep these features in mind:

1. The fielding range of the player is important. Some of your outfield "types" will be stunned when the ball is hit toward them, and unless the ball comes right to them, they won't have the presence of mind to move to the right or left to block it or retrieve it. They'll watch it go by and then as it rolls into the horizon they will commence to chase after it with enthusiasm, and vigor.

2. The relative courage level of a player could be very important as he may be required to get in front of the ball to prevent it from rolling into the horizon. Many young fielders will prefer blocking the ball by reaching at it from the side as it goes by which obviously decreases its chances of being stopped.

3. The ability to throw the ball back to the infield is important. A nicely retrieved ball in the outfield is accomplishing only half the goal. Some children have great problems with returning the ball to the infield. They've been known to "panic" and stand frozen with the ball held in the perfect throwing position for 10 seconds while the opposing base runners are clearing the bases. They've been known to field the ball cleanly, real and toss the ball excitedly over the other outfielders head into the horizon. They've been known to heave the ball all the way from their outfield position to 3 or 4 feet in front of them. They've been known to windup and release the ball on the backswing. They've also been known to throw the ball properly to the right base.

Being consistent with my observation that most
batters bat right handed, and hit toward left
field, it is important, therefore, to have the
best outfielders spread between center field and
left field. Of course there may be some
variations to this if the left side of your
infield is very strong, and your right side
needs bolstering.

USE THIS SPACE FOR YOUR NOTES

T - 3   COACHING THE INFIELD

In the rules we indicated to you that two defensive
coaches were allowed in the field during play. In
this section I'm going to advise on the best way to
take advantage of this rule and how to be a positive
influence on your fielders rather than a distraction.

The positioning of the coaches is very uniform from
team to team and game to game. The rules won't allow
any coach to position himself where he could inter-
fere with play, and more specifically won't allow him
to stand in the infield. This means the coaches can
roam anywhere they want beyond that boundary, or they
could even choose to sit on the bench and try to
influence play from there.

Most commonly, one coach will stand on the left side
of deep infield and the other will stand on the right
side.

Coaching the kids on defense is a very demanding job
and very essential to the success of the defense.
The important goals of the coaches are to:

1.   Keep the defensive players organized and
     positioned in their proper locations. But
     coaches are not allowed to touch a child in
     the game while the ball is in play. Thus
     he must keep him in the proper position
     through verbal direction only.

2.   Direct them in making the correct defensive
     play under the circumstances, and

3.   Teach them to anticipate the next play and
      prepare them to act on their own (which
      probably won't occur for most until after
      teeball.)

Each coach should be primarily responsible for a
specific segment of the defensive players. It is
most common for the coach stationed at deep shortstop
to be responsible for the fielders on the left side
of the field, and the other coach stationed at midway
between first and second base to be responsible for
the fielders on the rightside of the field. The
pitcher, since he stands in the middle of the coaching assignment zones, and since he is a very active
and involved player, will be covered by both coaches.
Overlapping of the coaching authority, however, can
be confusing to a player who is trying to listen for
the voice of a specific coach while he tries to
anticipate the ensuing play.

Instruction should always be given prior to the play
if possible, and repeated several times before the
ball is actually batted. For example, if a base
runner is on first with no other men on base, and the
batter coming up previously hit the ball toward the
shortstop, the instruction would be: "Let's get the
force-out at second base. Let's make an out on the
base runner when he goes to second base. Phil, don't
forget to cover the bag at second base. They may
throw it to you. Gary, if you get the ground ball
make an easy throw to Phil at second base; not too
high. Tom, throw to second base on this play. Throw
it to Phil for the out."

The coach could go on and instruct every player under
his auspices, and it wouldn't be uncommon if he did.
Remember the children really are not yet thinking
ahead for the next play. Most have all they can do
to figure out how to field the ball if it should come
to them, let alone figure out what to do with the
ball once they have it.

"Preventative" instructions, such as those examples
above, when given just prior to the next play,
negates some of the influence of inconsistent and
contradictory instructions coming from a variety of
sources once the play begins. (More about that latter)

Instruction should also be given during play. The
result, however, will vary between "effective", and
"adverse" depending upon the situation, the child,

24

and the excitement level of the game, fans and coach.

On many occasions the situation will change in the middle
of the play requiring the instruction to change in the
middle of the play.

Imagine this scenario:

> The parents are screaming in the stands from
> excitement; there's three "Mike's" on the team;
> the Mike you need is digging in the dirt; you
> have already prepared him for the play by
> telling him to throw to second for the force;
>
> The ball comes to him; you yell for the other
> Mike to cover second; the batter is named Mike,
> and his father is yelling for him to run to
> first; you tell Mike to throw to second, but
> he's still digging in the dirt until he hears,
> "Run to first" from the other Mike's dad and
> he's considering it;
>
> The ball goes through his legs, and the runners
> are advancing; Mike runs after it; the batter
> Mike stops at first, and his dad yells for him
> to go to second, but he doesn't, so his dad
> keeps yelling; in all the excitement the second
> baseman doesn't cover second; the original base
> runner heads alertly for third;
>
> Mike retrieves the ball, and follows precisely
> the instructions you gave him 10 seconds ago,
> and fires the ball to second base where there is
> no play, and where no fielder is standing.
>
> Coach, what's your next instruction?

I guarantee you that the above will be a frequent
occurrence in your teeball coaching career. Try to
enjoy it by seeing the humor in it. Be philosophical.
There is little you can do about it, but to keep
reinforcing the proper instruction and game stategy.
Step back now and then, and take notice and pleasure
in the progress your team is making.

Don't get upset if you find the children don't readily
accept your instruction during the play of the game.
Their concentration to the game will be very keen at
times, and non-existent at other times. And realize
that the children are translating your instructions
to images and ideas and preconceived concepts, and

this translation delays their response time. For example: If an outfielder retrieves a ball and you're instructing him, "second base!", he may not readily understand what "second base" means. Even though he knows what second base means, he still may not have interpreted what it means in the excitement of the moment.

In the above circumstance, while you're pleading with him to throw the ball to second base, he may fire a perfect shot to first base, or he may stand there immobile, and confused even though you may have put your instructions in the simplest terms.

The calmer you are in those kind of circumstances, the better he will understand what he is supposed to do as long as he can hear you. Sometimes, however, your control and composure may not provide the enthusiasm or audibility required in the circumstances. The child may react to the stongest stimulus which may be the other Mike's dad, not you. Be forceful, steady, loud enough, and not too excited, and you will get the message to him in the best possible manner.

Be consistent in your use of terminology in the instruction of what you want them to do. Begin this reinforcement of terminology in practice, and carry it to the game with you.

Among the things your defensive team must understand is your instructions relative to their fielding depth. Whether the players should play "deep", "shallow", or at "normal" depth may be an important instruction you'll want them to understand and react to quickly. Set up drills at practice saying "deep", and watch everybody shift back; "shallow", and watch everybody shift forward.

As a coach standing in the outfield you will find it difficult to recognize the next batter to be able to tell whether he is the one that hits the ball hard or without much power. All the batters will be wearing helmets, and it will be very difficult to distinguish them from other batters unless you have keen eyesight and a good view of their numbers. The recognition of where the batter hits the ball and how deep may not come until the last second requiring you to give immediate instructions to your fielders to "play deep" or "play in" or "shallow". They should be instructed to respond quickly, and never turn their

backs on the batter in the process. (It may happen
that you try to adjust a fielders depth at the last
moment only to find he is moving into position with
his back to the play and the ball on its way.)

USE THIS SPACE FOR YOUR NOTES

T - 4   ARRANGING THE BATTING ORDER AND
         RELATED STRATEGY

The arrangement of the batting order in teeball is
just as crucial to the success of the offense as it
is in regular baseball, however, the strategy used
and the criteria for batter sequence is quite
different.

Remember the rules state that all players on the team
will bat in each inning. And three outs in teeball
has no more significance than one out or two outs.

In regular baseball both sides have a batting order
of nine players. Not so in teeball. Before setting
your batting order in concrete you should check to
see if your team is going to have more or less
batters than your opponent. Though the sequence of
batters will always remain the same throughout the
game, the relationship to the lead-off batter could
change.

More batters. If your team has the same or more
batters than your opponent, you're going to establish
a batting order which won't change throughout the
game; Your lead-off batter will always be your lead-
off batter, and your last batter will always be your
last batter.

Fewer batters. However, if you have fewer batters
than your opponent you will be required to send to
bat as many batters as your opponent, and this will

change which batter leads off each inning. Although the established sequence of batters will not change the first batter of the new inning, for example, will not be the same batter you sent up to lead-off in the previous inning.

If your opponent has one more player than you do, you will bat your entire lineup plus your first batter for the second time in the inning. As a consequence, your second batter will become lead-off man in the second inning and bat twice in the second inning.

As you progress through the game, therefore, your first batter, then second, then third and so on will become your lead-off and clean-up batter. And the effect it will have on who bats last may be crucial to the outcome of an inning. You really don't want a weak batter to end the inning. If the bases are loaded, which could easily be the case, a weak batter could end the inning on a strike-out, or on a soft grounder back to the pitcher. This would be the equivalent of the defense earning four outs on one play as all the runners would be left stranded. And four outs is a lot of outs in teeball.

At a minimum your batting order strategy should be designed so that the last batter is one who has a good chance of hitting the ball through the infield, thus scoring all the runners on base, and maybe even himself. If your last batter is going to be different every inning, then you need to forecast what position will bat last and provide for it by assigning fairly good batters to those spots in the batting order.

Assuming your batting order is going to be constant for the entire game, that is, you and your opponent have an equal amount of players, or that you have more players than your opponent, the following is a summary of some of the key things to consider when setting your order.

1. Alternate strong and weak batters in the lineup if possible. This will keep the defense off balance, give your weak batters a better chance to get on base, and improve their chances of scoring.

2. Base running speed and aggressiveness must play an important part of the batting

29

sequence. You should not bat a very poor runner in front of a good runner. That sequence will just restrict the progress of the good runner, and maybe cause him to overrun the previous base runner.

3. Watch the batting order of fly ball hitters and ground ball hitters in relationship to specific base runners. There are some children who cannot grasp the technicality of the fly ball rule that states you have to hold-up until the ball is caught. These runners should bat in front of ground ball hitters if possible to prevent the related double play.

4. Anticipate the occupation of the bases in relationship to where the next batters normally hit the ball. This is especially true in the early part of the batting order where the occupation of bases are more easily predictable.

    For example; you would not want to have a poor runner at second, and a batter who usually hits slow grounders to shortstop or third base. For the batter who usually hits those kinds of balls, have him follow a batter who almost never gets to second off his own bat. If he's at first early in the inning with no one on base, then that batter can push him to second, then followed by a batter who hits to the right side of the field, or who hits a hard ball.

5. The lead-off batter in an inning, as in regular baseball, should be able to get on base a high percentage of the time and be a good aggressive base runner once he gets there. With no one in front of him he will be a distracting force on the bases opening the door and setting the stage for the progress of the rest of the batters.

    Remember too, the lead-off batter has the full concentration of the defense. If poor batter/runners are allowed to start off the inning, they could go out in sequence with no help in the form of distractions from good base runners. As in advanced baseball, base runners can help a batter get on base.

6.   Consider the right spot for a batter who
      has the ability to hit the ball to the
      right or left side. He could be placed in a
      position to help certain base runners.

7.   Make sure your last batter is not one who
      consistently hits back to the pitcher. As
      mentioned before, the pitcher will not
      have to make a play on him, under most
      Parks rules, and the inning will be over
      with a potential of many stranded base
      runners.

8.   For purposes of morale, rotate the last
      batter from game to game. Remember, if he
      does not hit a home run, he will never
      cross the plate. Scoring can be a glorious
      and rewarding thing for a child, and it
      wouldn't be fair to restrict one specific
      child from experiencing this just because
      he's the heaviest hitter on the team.

9.   Wait until the night before the game, or
      after your last practice to set your tenta-
      tive lineup. Your hitters will go in and
      out of batting streaks and your practices
      may give you a good indication of how your
      players are currently hitting. In addition
      children do get sick and miss games because
      of prior parent obligations. When you set
      the batting order early in the week, you're
      usually given many reasons during the week
      for changing it.

10.   Take batting practice before every game.
      Don't tire the children out with too much
      practice, but give them just enough to get
      their muscles warm, and their eye-hand
      coordination in tuned.

Now let's assume that you show up to the game with a
team that has _less_ ballplayers than your opponent.
Normally that can range between one to three players.

      In our example, the opponent has arrived at the
      game with 12 players, and you only have nine.
      (Don't get worried, typically it's the poorer
      players who don't show for the games. The
      better ones, whose parents are happy with their
      child's involvement and glory, usually see to it

that their child makes the game.) In setting the batting lineup you must be aware that every third batter is going to end up batting last or cleanup in one of the three or four innings you will play.

If you play four innings, your first cleanup batter is going to be hitting cleanup twice. Therefore, I would recommend having your strongest batter bat third. He will bat last in the 12th position of the first and fourth innings. Following the mathematics of this, your 6th and 9th batters should be good ones too as they will bat last in the second and third innings.

The same mathematics and related strategy apply if you have one or two _less_ players. With two or three less players, you are still able to alternate good with poorer batters near your cleanup positions.

The worst situation to be in is to have <u>one</u> less player since one less player will change the cleanup position by only one batter each inning forcing you to consider placing four good batters in succession at the beginning of the order to assure that a good batter will bat last all four innings.

For example; if you have 11 players, and your opponent 12, your first batter is going to bat twice the first inning and his last at bat that inning will be at the cleanup position. In the next inning your second batter will leadoff the inning and also bat last, and so on. It therefore behooves you to have good batters in the first through fourth positions. But good batters are usually hard to come by and you would not want to leave the remaining part of the batting order void of good hitters.

In other words, of your eleven players you could expect five of them to be pretty good hitters. If you bat four in succession at the beginning of the order, that will only leave one good batter to intersperse throughout the remaining six batters.

One other horrible occurence, which is almost an unmentionable, could subvert the planned efficiency of your strategic batting order. And that horrible occurence is "the late arrival".

What if, in the immediate example above, you
decide to place four of your five good batters
in the first, second, third and forth batting
positions figuring these batters will bat
cleanup in the first, second, third and fourth
innings.

The game starts and way across the other side of
the park, you see your 12th player racing to the
game. That means both sides will have the same
amount of players, and you won't have to have
different batters as cleanup each inning. But
since the game has already started your lineup
is officially set, and that means the little man
running across the field is going to be your
cleanup batter in every inning.

A similar problem could arise in the case where the
teams have the same number of players to start with,
say ten, and after setting the batting orders and
starting the game the other team has a late arrival
which will require you to bat one additional batter
each inning, therefore throwing your cleanup batter
alignment out of kilter.

USE THIS SPACE FOR YOUR NOTES

The importance of coaching the proper physical fundamentals cannot be overemphasized. The form developed
in youth may have a long-term impact on a childs
ability to compete and enjoy that sport.

The fundamentals of "strategy" have a different level
of importance. Strategy changes continually with the
situation at hand, and the potential of the athletes.
A wrong strategy taught to a young child can be
overcome without physical or permanent harm.   The
wrong strategy may even be forgotten. If the
physical fundamentals are taught improperly, they
could hurt a child's individual progress, hurt him
physically, and be much more difficult to overcome.

A lack of familiarity with the physical fundamentals
should neither inhibit, nor prevent an amateur coach
from instructing his players to the best of his
ability. There is a true shortage of coaches and the
worst thing that can happen is for a child not to
have a coach at all. If you want to coach and have
the interest in doing a good job, this book will give
you the tools you'll need to teach to the children
the physical fundamentals.

Coaching the fundamentals of throwing, catching,
batting, and running are significantly different from
coaching the strategies of the offense and the defense.
No matter how good your strategy is in the other
parts of the game, if the kids haven't learned some
of the basic physical fundamentals, the execution of

your strategy will be inconsistent and poor.

Since it is recognized that teeball is coached by
parents who frequently have a minimal amount of baseball experience, and a minimal amount of time to
conduct practices, you are going to be forced to be
very efficient in teaching the physical fundamentals.

It's a big responsibility in the time allotted, and
you'll probably be too hard on yourself and the kids
if you're the type who has high aspirations of mold-
ing the children into a well oiled machine. Take my
advice and don't take the responsibility entirely
upon yourself. Share it with the kids and share it
with the parents. Give them homework. Try to get
the dad's and mom's involved. Talk to the parents
about the child's form, and let them know what your
ideas are on how to improve or correct it. Give them
assignments on evening and weekend practices. But at
the same time, don't expect an olympic effort. The
kids and their parents will only invest so much of
their time and effort into teeball. Be realistic
about your expectations. You'll be just as successful if you do and you'll enjoy it a lot more.

Before teaching the children how to throw properly,
one must realize that their lack of physical strength
and coordination is going to detract significantly
from their ability to emulate the fundamental form of
an adult baseball player.

For example, a child's hands are so small that you
cannot expect them to hold the ball with the normal
"two-fingered" grip used by more advanced hardball
players. Depending upon the strength and size of
their hands, you may have to allow them to use a
three-fingered, or four-fingered grip.

Once you have shown them the proper way, allow them
to use the way that seems most in line with their
size, strength and coordination. If it feels
comfortable to them, it may be the right way for them
to do it.

As they grow they will also grow into the more
advance way of performing the physical fundamentals.
Switching to the two-fingered grip, for example, will
come natural to them as their hands grow, and they
discover they can throw faster, farther and with more
control.

The following are some of the most important fundamentals of <u>throwing overhand</u>:

1.   The ballplayer must hold the ball firmly.
     He must begin control of the ball where he
     initially comes in contact with it, in the
     palm of his hand. A firm grip does not
     mean stiff and rigid. A two, three or a
     four fingered grip, as mentioned above, is
     appropriate depending upon the size and
     strength of the child's hands. (See the
     example in figure T-5 a.)

2.   The throwers body should be in balance with
     the knees bent, anticipating a stride
     directly toward the target.

     If he has just fielded the ball, small,
     quick steps should be used to put him in a
     position of balance for the throw. (Left,
     right pick up the ball. Left, right
     throw.)

3.   He should raise his throwing hand up over
     his shoulder, away from his head.

     Some advanced teeballers will reach back
     more than they reach up, and that's O.K.
     but many will have a tendency to push the
     ball instead of throw it, and by raising
     the ball above the shoulders, and away from
     the head makes it easier to throw and not
     push. (See the example in figure T-5 b.)

     A baseball is supposed to be released by
     the thumb and allowed to roll out of the
     hand up toward the finger tips, and then
     from the ends of the fingers slung toward
     the target. This last-second slinging
     motion will usually cause the hand to come
     forward, breaking at the wrist in a
     flipping action.

     (An excellent drill to promote this
     "slinging" or "flipping" motion is to ask
     your players to hold the ball up in the air
     at the release point, and without moving
     their arms cock the wrist back, and flip
     the ball forward off the ends of the
     fingers, following through with the hand
     and breaking at the wrist. (See the
     examples in figures T-5 c, and T-5 d.)

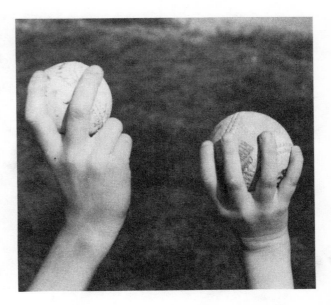

T-5 a.   Different size hands require different grips.

T-5 b.   The throwing arm should be
raised above the shoulder.

T-5 c.   Cock the wrist back.

T-5 d.   Flip the ball with the wrist
           holding the forearm still.

4. The thrower should then begin to turn his
    body away from the target, to the right if
    he is right-handed, while keeping his eyes
    on the target, keeping his arm cocked in
    the throwing position.

5. Then his body must begin its quick twist or
    pivot toward the target followed by the
    swinging of the throwing arm toward the
    target.

    The turning or pivoting of the body will
    not only help the player get speed on the
    ball, but will also help protect his arm as
    he matures.

    One way to communicate the need for this
    pivoting requirement is to tell the thrower
    that he has an imaginary "star" on the
    outside of each sleeve just below the
    shoulder. As the thrower pivots back
    before the throw he should end up with the
    star on the left sleeve facing the target,
    and the star on the right sleeve facing
    away from the target. When he completes
    his pivot, throw and follow through the
    star on his right sleeve should be facing
    the target, with the star on his left
    sleeve facing away from the target.
    (See examples in figures T-5 e, and T-5 f.)

6. If right-handed, his left leg should
    already be striding toward the target. The
    length of the stride should be designed to
    give momentum toward the target without
    losing balance, nor an inordinate amount of
    time. (See the example in figure T-5 g.)

7. His whole body then should be moving toward
    the target, with his feet planted, flowing
    smoothly into the complete follow-through.

8. The left gloved hand, if a right-handed
    thrower, can be swung out away from the
    body to aid in maintaining the balance of
    the throw.

9. The thrower should quickly end up in
    balance with knees bent facing the target,
    and ready for the next eventuality. (See
    the example in figure T-5 h.)

T-5 e.   The left shoulder faces the target.

T-5 f.   The right shoulder faces the target.

T-5 g.   The left leg strides toward the target.

T-5 h.   After the throw, get in balance and ready.

One observation I have made is that some good throwers seem to throw more poorly when playing catch with a teammate than when they are playing catch with the coach. One cause of this is that children do not want to hurt each other, and therefore will take a lot off the ball in trying to make it easier to catch. This could cause the good thrower to push the ball instead of fling it, and as a result he could get into bad habits just because he thinks he is throwing to a fragile target.

The underhand toss is an important throwing form in teeball. The players should learn how to reach the target with an underhand toss when the distance to the target is under 15 feet.

It may be frightening to a child to have a player field a ball within 15 feet of him, and wind up with an overhand motion that looks like the ball will be thrown right through him. You will find the target ducking, flinching or going through other gyrations in fear that he may get hit with the ball in a place other than the pocket of his glove. The easy underhand toss can remedy this problem.

The underhand toss should be taught similar to the form used in bowling where the body pivots back a little with the arm going down, with stiff wrist, back beyond the torso, and then pivoting slightly forward toward the target. In the follow through the stiff arm and nearly stiff wrist should swing forward with the ball released at belly level (away from the body) in a nice easy arc to the target. (See examples in figure T-5 i, and T-5 j.)

T-5 i.   No bending of the arm and wrist
          to start the underhand toss.

T-5 j.   The arm and wrist remain stiff
          at the end of the underhand toss.

Catching a ball hit into the air will probably be the
most difficult thing for a coach to teach and the
child to accomplish. The fundamentals of catching a
ball in the air are rather simple. As to whether the
ball is caught or not depends a lot upon the fielder's
visual judgement, agility, eye-hand coordination,
overall coordination, speed, range and concentration.
That certain ability to see a ball in flight and be
able to judge where it's going could be the key
element of catching a ball, and it is the one element
that can't be taught.

Coach, you can end up teaching all the proper fundamentals of catching, but if your players don't have
that ability to judge where the ball is going, your
coaching effort won't yet pay off. But don't let
yourself get impatient, or frustrated in this aspect
of the game. Catching, like many other areas of a
childs ability is going to progress only through
practice, experience, and maturation. And one thing
that will be consoling about the whole thing is that
the other coaches will be in the same boat.

There are some important fundamentals, however, you
can teach in the game of catching that can help your
players improve their performance and put them into a
position ready for rapid improvement. The areas that
I list below, you may note, relate first to preparedness and choice of equipment, and then the physical
fundamentals of catching.

Preparedness and choice of equipment:

1. Make sure the child has a glove that fits
    him properly. One that is too large or too
    heavy can make it difficult for him to
    control and catch. And watch the length of
    the glove fingers. A short-fingered glove
    is easier to control. A long-fingered
    glove can be unwieldy and leads to one
    handed fielders.

    There are many inexpensive gloves available,
    all leather or partial leather, that can be
    purchased for under $15 that easily satisfy
    all the requirements of teeball.

2. Pay close attention to the stiffness of the
    glove. Some gloves are made completely of
    vinyl and in cool weather become very
    stiff. Stiff pockets repel the ball
    causing it to bounce out more readily than
    you'd want. I personally recommend an all-
    leather glove.

    And make sure it's leather on the front,
    back and inside. An all leather glove, if
    maintained properly, will end up being a
    lot more pliable and the players ability to
    catch the ball will be greatly enhanced.

    By the way, one way to tell if it is a
    leather glove or not, other than smell, is
    to scratch the glove in various spots with
    your fingernail. Leather will show the
    scratch marks, vinyl probably won't.

3. If it is a leather glove, make sure that it
    is well broken-in and oiled. Gloves that
    are brand new do not necessarily take
    months to break-in. One successful method
    that I found in breaking in a new glove was
    to:

    a. Soak the new glove in warm water
        for about 5 minutes.

    b. Remove the glove from the water
        and lightly towel-dry.

    c. Place the glove on cement, pocket-
        side up, and pound the pocket with

the large end of the bat for
about another 5 minutes. Don't
pound so hard so as to damage the
leather, or stitching, but hard
enough to begin seeing a break-
down in the stiffness of the
glove. Pound it in a way that
helps form the pocket of the
glove.

d.   Then oil the glove thoroughly on
the outside, back, front, seams,
and on the inside where the hand
goes.

e.   Finally, place a leather hardball
in the glove pocket, and wrap the
glove tightly around it with
string letting it set up in the
closet for two or three days
drying.

Your final product will be a
broken-in glove that took you a
few days to accomplish the job
most ballplayers would take all
Summer to do.

4.   During practices and during the games make
sure your players "pat" their gloves frequently. This helps mold the pocket making
it deeper and softer to receive the ball.
Show the players how to pound the glove
with their fists so that it doesn't hurt
their hands. And especially remind them to
do this every time they take the field
during a game. A few pats of the glove can
make a big difference in their defensive
performance for that inning.

5.   Check to see that your players are wearing
their gloves properly. It is not incon-
ceivable that they could be placing their
fingers in the wrong finger slots. It
isn't always necessary that a child place
each one of his fingers in the normally
designated finger slot, because in some
cases it is more comfortable, and one has
more control of the glove if a variable fit
is used. The coach's job under these circumstances is to make sure the child is

informed of the proper way to wear a baseball glove, and that the glove is worn in a
way that submits to the control of the
hand.

6. Make sure they maintain their gloves
    properly. Show them how and where to
    place their gloves when they come in from
    the field. A mistreated glove, one for
    example that is thrown on the ground at the
    end of the dugout, will dry out and stiffen
    quicker than one that is treated well.

Success in accomplishing most of the physical fundamentals of catching a thrown or batted ball depends
significantly on the player's judgement, eye-hand
coordination and lack of fear of the ball. Most
infields you play on will be poorly kept-up and bad
hops will be common

Since the ball is lighter and softer than a regular
baseball and since the batters never hit the ball too
hard, the chance of a serious injury is minimal.
However, some balls will be hit hard enough to stun
or bruise a player, and you should be sympathetic and
understanding. It is not the time yet to make tough
he-men out of them.

The physical fundamentals of fielding a ground ball
are somewhat different from that of catching a fly ball.
Consequently, we will review the fundamentals of each
separately and start with fielding ground balls.

1. Keep the body and glove low on ground
    balls. When coaching, try to exaggerate
    this position. Make sure the fielders bend
    their knees. Show them how to keep very
    low to the ground, even able to slap their
    glove right on top of the dirt infield.
    Balls will much more frequently go under
    their gloves than over their gloves.
    (See the example in figure T-6 a.)

    Most of the time a player will be waiting
    for a ground ball with his glove hand a
    foot or two above the ground anticipating
    to go down for it if it's necessary. He
    doesn't realize than the arms and hands can

47

come up for a ball much quicker than they can go down for one.

2. The fielders feet should establish a wide base (feet wide apart but not off balance) from which to begin fielding a ground ball. The left foot should be a little forward of the right, with the right toe level with the left instep.

3. The arms should extend the glove and hand out away from the body so that the eye-hand contact can have its positive influence on telling the player exactly where the ball is in relationship to the glove. If a fielder cannot see his glove because it is too close to his body, then he may have a difficult time lining it up on the same plane as the ball. Have your fielders keep their gloves out in front of them so they can keep the glove and ball on the same plane.

    The ball should be caught toward the glove side of the body.

4. For balls caught below the waist, the heel of the glove should be up with the fingers pointing down.

    When the ball bounces above the waist, the glove should be turned around with the fingers pointing up and the heel down. (See the example in figure T-6 b.)

5. The eyes should try to see the ball as soon as it becomes visible whether right off the end of the bat, or just out of the hand of the thrower. The greater the concentration of the fielder on the where-a-bouts of the ball, the better his chances of seeing it, figuring out where it is going and feeling comfortable about the ball coming at him.

6. The fielder's eyes should watch the ball travel all the way into his glove. It may be years later (and maybe never) before the blur of a close ball can really be seen clearly by him, but impress upon him that if he watches the ball right into the pocket of the glove, his fielding will

T-6 a.   Catch the bottom of the ball
           on low grounders.

T-6 b.   Glove fingers point away from the belt.

improve immensely, and he will eventually
be able to see the ball better. His eye
image ability will quicken, and his eye
memory image will calculate the geometrics
of the catch more accurately.

7.   The glove hand and throwing hand should
work together, especially on balls hit
directly to the fielder, in securing the
ball in the glove and preparing to throw.
The glove should take the impact of the
ball and fold somewhat around the ball.
Then the bare hand must act as a lid and
trap the ball in the pocket, and prepare
for the quick throw.

8.   A muffed ball should be pursued without
delay. Feeling sorry or angry at oneself
for bobbling the ball is no reason to cease
trying to field the ball and complete the
play.

Because of a lack of coordination on the
fielder's part, or even because of the lack
of a good fielder's glove many balls will
hit the glove and fall out. Teach the
players how to retrieve the ball with their
bare throwing hand and still make the play.
Make sure your players don't give up on the
ball. The ball is still in play, and
because of frequent poor base running your
fielder may be given ample time to still
make the play.

9.   Children must look for a loose ball at
their feet with their eyes not their hands.
You will find that the children have a
tendency to look up toward the runner while
trying to feel for the ball with their hand
or glove without looking for it. Emphasize
and demonstrate the need to forget the
runner while searching for the ball, and
then, once the ball is found, and is secure
in their hand or glove, to seek out the
runner and make the play if feasible.
(See example in figure T-6 c.)

10.   Have some fielder always backup the play.
If the ball is hit to the shortstop,
perhaps the left fielder should back him up
in case the ball goes by him. If the ball

is hit through the infield to an outfielder, make sure the outfielders closest
to the ball are running to backup the fielder
in the line with the ball.

Balls thrown back to the pitcher must be
backed up by the infielder most directly in
line with the throw, and behind the pitcher.

The fielder backing up the intended catcher
should leave himself enough room to be able
to see the ball after it has been missed.
If he stands too close, there is a good
possibility that the backup fielder won't
have time to react to the play and will
miss the ball too. The recommended distance
for backing up is between 15 and 20 feet
behind the original fielder.

Catching fly balls is quite an exceptional thing for
children of this age group. Usually it requires two
improbabilities occurring at the same time. The two
improbabilities are; 1. that the ball be hit gently
into the air directly toward an infielder, and 2.
that the infielder be one of the few who have the
ability to catch fly balls. Nonetheless, there are a
couple of things that can be coached to increase the
possibility of a child catching a fly ball.

1. Make sure your players keep their glove
   hand out away from their body, and up high
   so that they can see the ball and the glove
   at the same time upon making the catch.
   When the eye-hand coordination combines with
   a little experience, it will produce someone who rather frequently catches the ball.
   (See the example in figure T-6 d.)

2. Teach your players not to instinctively run
   up on balls hit into the air. Most players
   misjudge the ball thinking it will be shorter
   than it ends up being. The worse thing
   that can happen is to have a ball hit over
   a players head. If it drops in front of
   him he can still make a play. If it goes
   over his head, it's his backup man's ball,
   if there is one.

T-6 c.   The eyes find the loose ball at the feet.

T-6 d.   Catch the ball out and away from the body.

3. When running for a fly ball, the fielder
   should not extend his arm and glove to
   catch the ball until the ball is in
   catching range. Running a distance with
   the arm extended merely slows down the
   runner and puts him off balance.

USE THIS SPACE FOR YOUR NOTES

The batting swing is one of the areas of teeball that is most like advanced baseball. Most of the funda- mentals that produce a successful baseball hitter are the same fundamentals that are required to produce a successful teeball hitter. One important difference, however, is that since there is no pitch, the tee- baller has less elements to consider... he always knows the speed of the pitch (stationary), and where it will cross the plate (dead center).

Just because teeball rules have taken away the guessing game from the batter by eliminating the pitch, the challenge of hitting the ball well still exists. The challenge is gaining control of the bat in order to hit the ball where and how it should be hit in the circum-stances. Hitting it either on the fly, or on the ground; hitting it through the hole instead of at someone; or hitting it with power and authority instead of weakly, are all elements of performance that can be accomplished once the funda- mentals are learned and applied.

A good place to start with the children is to have them show you how they bat. This will quickly let you know the kinds of things you'll need to teach, and it will give you a bench mark to their progress.

You may quickly find while they are demonstrating their ability to bat that some of the children do not know how to hold the bat properly. A right-handed batter (one whose right shoulder faces away from the field), must have his left hand wrapped around the bat closest to the nub of the bat. The right hand is then wrapped around the bat above but not on-top-of the other hand. There is no interlocking finger thumb requirement as in some golf grips. The hands are placed below and above each other, and most of the time in a fairly close arrangement. (See the example in figure T-7 a.)

A left-handed batter will hold the bat with his right hand closest to the nub, and left hand above it.

Get the players in a group and explain to them in chrono-logical sequence most of what they have to know about batting. Start by introducing them to the "tee", and how it is positioned over the plate; and how it is adjustable. Show them the batters box and how they will position themselves in relationship to the ball on the tee.

Show them the foul lines from the view of a batter, and explain all the related rules of a fair and foul ball.

Place the ball on the tee and show them the "sweet" spot out toward the end of the bat where it is best to hit the ball, and show them where the surface of the ball should be hit with the bat. Remind them that missing the ball is a strike even if they hit the tee.

Show them the general nature of the swing, and then let them show you what they can do. Anymore time spent in demonstration and you'll lose them in fantasy land.

As they start hitting you'll notice that they will be willing to hit the ball off the tee at whatever height the tee is placed. Explain to them the importance of setting the height of the ball that feels most comfortable to them, and help them decide when they are most comfortable. The best overall height should be about six to eight inches below the top of the shoulders.

Here's some important hitting fundamentals you can teach them.

1. Help the child adjust his body stance so
    that his feet are comfortably placed under
    his shoulders. Make sure he has good body
    balance from his stance through the end of
    his swing. Knees bent a little for control
    and balance; body also bent a little at the
    waist with the upper torso and head leaning
    a little toward the batters box on the
    other side of the plate. The heels, then,
    should come up a little and be able to
    bounce off the ground. (See the example in
    figure T-7 b.)

2. Before placing a bat in the hands of your
    ball players have them all practice
    stepping toward the pitcher or toward the
    direction you want them to hit the ball.

    As a drill set the players all in one line,
    arms length apart, facing you. Have them
    take their batting stances and with your
    back toward them stride toward an imagi-
    nary pitcher or tee, and have them imitate
    you a number of times. Look around now and
    then to see if they are all striding toward
    the target, or have an assistant coach make
    sure they are. Stride... stride...stride.
    They won't even need a bat in their hands,
    but they should hold their hands up as if
    they do.

    Learning how to stride into a ball which
    actually transfers energy from the feet,
    legs and torso through the shoulders, arms
    and hands to the bat, will especially help
    the under-developed or weak child deliver
    more power into his swing.

3. Now put a bat in their hands applying the
    grip form mentioned earlier in this
    chapter. It's o.k. if the children move
    their hands up and down the bat in rela-
    tionship to the nub. When they're feeling
    strong and powerful they will want to swing
    from the end of the bat, and when they
    don't feel so great they'll want to choke
    up a little. Make sure, however, that they
    know these options are available to them.

T-7 a.   Grip the bat properly.

T-7 b.   Body balance in the batters box.

On some occasions, however, you may want to
dictate how much they should "choke up" on
the bat. In advanced baseball the speed or
style of the pitcher may influence a batter
on choking. The weight of the bat should
almost never be a determining factor. If a
batter chokes-up because the bat is too
heavy, he should use a lighter bat. The
exception is if there is no bat available
that is lighter than the one being used.
So if the child is struggling because the
bat is too heavy, and no lighter one is
available, have him choke up a little.

4. Make sure their stance in relationship to
    the plate and ball is set-up so that they
    are several inches back and to the right of
    the tee for a right-handed batter. You
    don't want the ball directly in front of
    them as they face the plate from the
    batters box. (See example in figure T-7 c.)

    In advanced baseball the bat should come in
    contact with the ball out in front of the
    plate, not over it. But in teeball the tee
    apparatus is designed to set on top of the
    plate instead of out in front of it. This
    position may force the batter to hit the
    ball directly in front of him instead of
    beyond that point to the left of his left
    shoulder. Thus to compensate, the batter
    must move his stance toward the back of the
    batters box so that the natural point of
    impact with the ball takes advantage of the
    full swing which includes the stride, arms
    swing and the breaking of the wrists.

5. Make sure they push with their back foot as
    they are striding into the swing.

    Many children shift too much of their
    weight onto their front foot and pick up
    their back foot as they swing. Ideally,
    their weight is shifting to the front foot,
    but the back foot is still carrying sub-
    stantial weight while pushing the body
    toward the target. The back foot should
    not be lifted off the ground during any
    part of the swing, but pivoted. The

sensation for the back foot would be as if
the batter is twisting his foot to squash a
bug. If the foot does lift, the batter is
probably off balance and not striding
properly. (See the example in figure T-7 d.)

6.   Now that they have the body movement some-
      what in the proper sequence and direction,
      give them a lightweight bat. The kids all
      seem to want to pick up bats that are too
      heavy for them. Discourage this by identi-
      fying small, lightweight bats, perhaps 26
      or 27 inches in length, and only keep those
      lightweight bats available for them to use.

      You will find their swings much more power-
      ful and accurate when they use a lighter
      bat. A heavy bat may even force them to
      change their stance and swing to compensate
      for the additional weight.

7.   Their arms and hands should be up and away
      from their chests in their stance position.
      The hands should be to the right of the
      rear shoulder; elbows slightly up.
      (See the example in figure T-7 e.)

      This is done to prepare them for the rela-
      tive position of their hands, arms and bat
      at the point of impact with the ball.
      Thinking of their torso as the fulcrum, the
      greatest speed in the chain that links the
      batter to the sweet spot is achieved at the
      end of the bat. As the bat and arms pro-
      gress away from the body even greater speed
      is attained; add that to the assistance of
      gravity in a slightly downward swing of the
      bat, and one has generated considerable bat
      speed.

      The first movement of the swing is to move
      the hands a few inches away from the ball
      toward the backstop as the front foot
      begins the stride. Then the weight begins
      to transfer as outlined in section 5 above.
      The swing should also include taking the left
      hand to the ball. The head should be down
      in the middle of the "V" of the arms with a
      level two-eyed look at the ball.

T-7 c.   To make contact with the ball ahead of
the lead shoulder, set up deep in the box.

T-7 d.   Squash the bug
with the ball of the back foot..

If a batters stance includes arms and hands that are too close, and low, the swing arc will be reduced thus reducing bat speed, and if they swing up at the ball, gravity will act against bat speed. Of course there are other reasons why a batter shouldn't uppercut a ball.

For those batters who may have an extreme uppercut problem (which is common at this age) here's a drill:

..Place a target in the infield dirt about 20 feet in front of the plate, and have the batter try to hit that target with the batted ball. The only way they'll be able to hit it is by swinging down on the ball. (See the example in figure T-7 f.)

8. Make sure they're swinging the bat, not pushing it.

Conceptually, "swinging" the bat is like throwing the bat at the ball. The arms and hands are extended away from the body; the bat is swung from a position behind the right shoulder; the wrists break fiercely at just about the point of impact; and the follow-through pulls the torso all-the-way around.

If the children are "pushing" the bat, little bat speed will be attained. A good drill for those that are pushing the bat is for them to hold the bat high, and back away from their body with the wrists cocked back or bent so that the bat is pointing back over their shoulder behind their right ear. Then have them throw their bat at the ball a few times to get their wrists breaking, and the swinging motion understood. (See the example in figure T-7 g.)

The swing should start from the bat position held up and to the right of the body and back toward the umpire in the batting stance. Watch out for the child that sets-up properly, then proceeds to move the bat toward the ball and "punches" at the ball. The bat throwing drill can help this child.

T-7 e.   The first move from here is
away from the target...coiling for the swing.

T-7 f.   Hit the target in front of the pitching
circle to overcome swinging up on the ball.

Another drill to help a child stop punching at the ball from a close distance is the following ..Have the child take his stance with the bat held up and to the right of his rear shoulder, then stand behind him and hold the end of the bat. While he is looking at the target, have him pull the bat out of your grip toward the target. This makes him understand where the initial force is to be generated in the swing, and it also strengthens the muscles necessary to start the swing back there. (See the example in figure T-7 h.)

If the batter is one that was punching at the ball with a partial swing, he would have probably swung more accurately using his old method than the full swing method you've just taught him. But in time, and not too much time, he'll be hitting the ball with precision as well as power.

9.   Strive eventually for a level swing. To overcome their extremes you may have to coach the opposite extreme, but this has got to be temporary.

The swing you prepare them for must be the swing that is on the same plane as the (eventual) pitch. This will enhance the childs ability to make contact with the ball. Admittedly, in teeball, it is not so critical to coach a level swing because the non-pitched ball is stationary, thus there is no "flight" path or plane of the ball. The law of averages, therefore, are not improved by swinging in the same plane as the ball is traveling. Nonetheless, his whole body movement, and his future perfor-mance may depend upon him learning to swing level.

10.   Directional hitting is the next thing to be taught.

Most of your players will have a tendency to hit the ball directly back to the pitcher. In teeball, the pitcher is usually one of the best fielders on the

63

T-7 g.   Have them throw the bat mostly
with their wrists to appreciate the whip like action.

T-7 h.   The batter can "feel" where the swing must
begin.   No "pushing" allowed.

team, and balls hit back to him will stand the best chance of producing outs. As a consequence, directional hitting will have to be taught at a very early part of the season.

You'll find that directional hitting will be a very easy concept for some children to pick up, and yet for others, it will be very difficult.

Some will move their feet and stance around just a little, and hit the ball 40 feet from where they were hitting it before. Others will move their bodies all the way around, and end up hitting the ball pretty close to where they hit it before they moved.

Basically, if you want a right-handed batter to hit the ball to left field, he must bat square in the batters box with his left foot striding a little toward the "bucket" or toward third base. In setting up, his feet should be deep in the box and close to the plate. (See the example in figure T-7 i.)

If you want him to hit the ball the other way, then he must move up in the box, front foot toward the inside line closest to the plate and the back foot about 12 inches away from the inside of the line. As he strides, he steps a little toward right field, keeps the bat open (faced), and swings away. (See the example in figure T-7 j.)

Directional hitting can also mean hitting the ball up or down. Some players can become quite adept at hitting easy fly balls over the pitchers head, and this may be something you should consider coaching later in the season.

11.   Don't worry about the other technicalities of batting such as the thumb positioning, the intricacies of breaking the wrists in the swing, the positioning of the elbow, chin, etc. Just try to correct the most

T-7 i.   Help the ball to left field with a step
in the same direction.

T-7 j.   Help the ball to right field with
a closed stance, open bat.

important thing that meets your eye at the
time, and correct it now. Demonstrate it
to the offender and to all the other
players who are watching. They'll pick up
on the things you're looking for though the
mistakes of their teammates.

You may find a child doing eight things
wrong. Just concentrate on correcting one
of them. That's about all he'll be able to
concentrate on...and you may find that by
correcting that one thing, three other
improvements will come along with it.

12.   No bunting.

In the leagues I coached bunting was discouraged but not prohibited. It basically
consisted of the batter swinging very
lightly at the ball with just enough force
to hit it beyond the batters foul circle.
This is a good offensive weapon because
many of the pitchers are not capable of
running up from the pitching circle,
fielding the ball cleanly, and throwing the
ball accurately to first base.

However, from the angle of "good sportsmanship" the rules and nature of the game tend
to suggest that premeditated bunting should
not be allowed. We've already pointed out
two important elements that support this
position.

        The first is that the pitcher has to
        be stationed inside the pitching
        circle until the ball is hit. So the
        rule forces him to remain distant from
        the batter he suspects is going to bunt.

        The second is that the game is
        normally played without a catcher.
        This is done for safety reasons,
        therefor I believe any situation that
        would contradict the lack of need of a
        catcher should be prohibited. But the
        cincher is that we would not want our
        children playing first base and third
        base to be put in a situation where
        they may be asked to move up on a

batter who may fake a bunt and hit
away placing the unsuspecting fielders
in immediate danger.

I don't believe in coaching or using the
bunting tactic in teeball.

USE THIS SPACE FOR YOUR NOTES

The most important difference from the base running
of young teeballers and advanced baseball players is
that teeballers don't respond to the base coach's
instructions as quickly as the advanced players do.
An instruction may have to be repeated several times
before the child responds, and when he finally
responds, it fre- quently is too late. Typically, a
base running instruction given during the game, may
not "sink in" until a few seconds after it has been
given, and the base runner may respond to the
instruction after it has already been countermanded.

Your base running "control" may go something like this:

Little Elmer is on second base and you're
coaching him from the third base box. You're
preparing him to run as soon as the ball is hit
by the next batter and you know the chances of
doubling up on a pop fly are slim, and Elmer
needs all the running advantage he can get. The
ball is hit and Elmer takes off from second,
but its a lazy pop fly to the best fielder, the
pitcher. Nonetheless, Elmer's bearing down on
third base while you're screaming at him to
return to second. He's almost at third now and
is beginning to get the idea that he must return
to second, and quickly.

But then, the pitcher drops the fly ball. So as
Elmer is headed back to second after being
almost on top of the third base bag, you begin

yelling at him (over the crowd noise) to stop and proceed to third.

One other element now comes into the picture ...the batter, who is an aggressive little base runner, has kept running during all this and is bearing down on second base. Elmer sees the batter headed toward the same base he is headed and decides that he is no longer in a teeball game, but in a race to second base.

Meanwhile you've gotten quite excited and so has your first base coach. He's trying to get the batter back to first, and by this time you've decided it's best for Elmer to continue on to second and stay there, but then the pitcher picks up the fly ball he's just dropped and in an attempt to get the runner headed for second throws it wildly into the outfield....

Now it's time to tell Elmer to hurry to third, but he is reeling in the glory that he beat the batter to second, and you can't get his attention. The batter meanwhile has picked-up the first base coaches plea to get back to first so that Elmer would be safe at second, and has returned un-triumphantly back to first. Meanwhile both base coaches seeing the ball still rolling in the outfield are now screaming for the runners to advance to the next base......

I think you get the picture. I won't tell you how it came out, because you'll have a situation just like it when you coach and you'll see how it turns out first-hand.

Don't be discouraged; by the end of the season you will find quite an improvement in their base running ability, and responsiveness to the base coaching instructions.

The childrens' response time delay, of course, is very normal. Throughout your coaching experience with children at this level you must remember they are translating the words you use in your instruction to words and images that they understand. And they only react after they have completed their trans- lation and the instruction has become meaningful to them.

70

For example: We were coaching the kids concerning the care that has to be taken when running on a fly ball. After we practiced hitting fly balls, and running or not-running as the case may be for about 15 minutes, we brought the kids into a huddle, and re-emphasized "why" they shouldn't immediately run on most fly balls, and that they must wait to see if the ball would be caught, and listen for the base coach's instructions. We then asked if the children had any questions, and one player raised his hand and asked, "Coach, what is a fly ball?"

A "fly ball" is nomenclature common to baseball, but may not be words that are easily translatable to someone just entering baseball for the first time. If we had changed the instruction, from "Don't run on a fly ball.", to "Don't run when a ball is hit into the air.", we probably would have succeeded in our instruction much more readily.

Of course, it is also very natural for a coach to use common baseball terms such as "fly ball", "force out", "foul ball", etc., and assume the children understand what is being said. But they may not. I encourage using these terms because the children have to learn them, but perhaps initially they should be used in conjunction with a more definitive description.

The following are some important fundamentals in improving your teams base running performance.

1. Have all the children wear rubber cleats. Infields can be very compact and slippery, and traction is essential to their improved performance and safety.

2. The first place to start in teaching the art of base running is at home plate. Make sure they start running to first as soon after their bat has made contact with the ball as possible. Getting away from the plate immediately is absolutely essential. Don't allow them to watch the batted ball, or straighten their cap, or anything else but to get their balance and start running.

3. Many of the leagues require helmets be worn
    when batting and on the bases even though
    there is no pitched ball. The helmet is
    there to protect the runner on the bases.
    Make sure the children are instructed not
    to worry about the helmet when proceeding
    from one base to another. He may find the
    helmet is ill fitted, and it may easily
    fall off when running. The child should be
    coached to ignore the fallen helmet until
    he has reached a base and time-out has been
    called.

    The ill fitted helmet may effect them in
    other manners too. You may notice some
    children bowing their back and head in an
    unusual manner while running the bases, and
    they are doing it to create the least
    amount of bounce from their neck up so that
    the helmet won't fall off. Instruct them
    that it is O.K. if the helmet falls off and
    that it's more important that they get to
    the next base as fast as possible running
    with their natural form.

4. Upon approaching first base they should
    look for the first base coach's base
    running signals. The base coach should
    include different signals with verbal
    instructions. The signals are in reality
    visual aids for the children to easily
    understand what they are instructed to do.
    The signals should be simple and con-
    sistent. Here are the ones we used:

      a. For stopping at first....the first
         base coach faces the batter/base
         runner with the right hand and arm out
         straight at the runner with the hand
         bent up as in a policeman's stopping
         motion. The left arm should be out
         away from the body pointing at the
         first base dugout. (See the example
         in figure T-8 a.)

         This instructs a child to stop at
         first, but run through the bag, not
         stopping on the bag, and turn right
         into foul territory before slowing
         down and returning to the bag.

b. For turning at first....the first base coach merely points towards second with his right arm and hand.

   This instructs the base runner to make a turn at at first towards second, but not continue running to second.

c. For continuing on to second....the first base coach should point to second with his right hand and pinwheel his left arm. (See the example in figure T-8 b.)

   This instructs the base runner to run thru the bag at first, and continue to second unabated.

d. For stopping at second...the third base coach holds both hands out in front of him in the stopping motion.

e. For rounding second....the third base coach merely points towards left field.

   This instructs the runner to round second base, but not continue on to third.

f. For continuing on to third base....the third base coach pinwheels his right arm, while he waves the runner approaching second toward him with his left.

g For stopping at third base....the third base coach merely holds up both hands in the policeman's stopping posture while facing the runner.

   This instructs the runner to stop at third and stay on the bag (without sliding if possible).

h. For rounding third base....the third base coach points towards home with his right hand, while the left hand can be waving the runner toward third.

   This instructs the runner to round

T-8 a.　　A animated plea to stop at first base,
　　　　　but not immediately on the bag.

T-8 b.　　The left arm pinwheeling always tells the
　　　　　runner to keep running.

third base without stopping, and
continue toward home plate for a few
feet past third only.

    i. For continuing on to home....the third
      base coach pinwheels his left arm
      while pointing towards home with his
      right.

5. The base runners should be taught to run
straight to the next base.

The children can run a small hook upon
approaching first base to get them heading
toward second, but they won't be able to
make sharp turns like they're supposed to
if they are running hard. Nonetheless,
they should be instructed to keep as close
as possible to a straight line instead
making a big sweep toward the outfield.

6. Teach them that while on the base paths
they should try to locate the whereabouts
of the ball, but it should not be done in a
manner that distracts from their base running speed, direction or attention to the
base coach.

Knowing where the ball is gives them additional knowledge with which to make judgements as to how to proceed on the bases.

7. The base runner should be taught to look
for the next base coach as soon as possible.

For example, as the runner rounds first
base he should try to pick-up the location
of the ball while listening to the first
base coach behind him. Then halfway toward
second the runner should become aware of
what the third base coach wants him to do.
He should "pick-up" the third base coach
out of the corner of his eye while he is
running.

All this will seem quite confusing to the
young base runner. He has to look for the
ball, listen for the first base coach,

75

pick-up the third base coach, and keep an
eye on the bag ahead of him all at the same
time. But practicing these techniques from
the beginning will help make these elements
become automatic later in the season.

8. Instruct the children to touch all bases
    with a sizeable part of their foot. (See
    the example in figure T-8 c.)

    Advanced base runners use a small edge of
    the base as leverage in changing the direc-
    tion of their momentum and pushing them
    toward the next base. However, the coordi-
    nation and timing of teeballers is faulty.
    If their judgement is off a little, they
    will miss the base altogether. Thus, to
    compensate for this the coach should teach
    the objective of a direct hit.

    In addition, children don not need as much
    of a push from the base as do base runners
    in advanced baseball because their speed
    weight and inertia is significantly less.

9. The coach must distinguish for the kids the
    difference in the rules from being allowed
    to pass the bag at first off the hit and
    still be safe after the tag, from not being
    safe at second and third when tagged after
    coming off the bag.

10. The best way to prevent from overrunning
    the bag is to have the base runner slow
    down just before he arrives at the bag.
    You'll may lose some close plays, but very
    few.

    I don't recommend sliding to prevent over-
    running the bases at the flyweight level,
    but some advanced players may be taught how
    to slide at the mightymite level. In
    general, however, I don't think sliding is
    necessary or advisable at this young age.

11. Bring to the attention of the children the
    need for them to differentiate the base

coachs' voices from those of their parents
and game fans. They should be listening,
obviously, for only the coaches.

12. Teach the base runners how to help the
     batter, and how to help other base runners.
     This will be a difficult feature of base
     running to accomplish especially at the
     flyweight level, but it is one that will
     eventually pay numerous dividends.

     For example, a runner on third base can
     frequently help a batter get to first on a
     ball hit back to the pitcher or third base-
     man. He can do this by making the fielder
     think for a moment that he must make a play
     on himself not the batter. Sometimes just
     an instant hesitation can give the batter
     time enough to get an advantage in his race
     to first.

     But to do this the base runner must come
     off the "security" of the bag, be seen, and
     act as if he intends to advance home. He
     must be prepared to scurry back to safety
     as soon as necessary, but not too soon.

     If the fielder ignores the base runner then
     he is in excellent position to advance to
     the next base as soon as the fielder re-
     leases the ball in his throw to the other
     base.

13. When a base runner is stationary on a bag
     waiting for the next play, he should always
     be facing the infield. His right foot
     should always be the advanced foot. His
     left foot should always be on the bag.
     Watch for this, because many of your base
     runners will setup improperly. (See the
     example in figure T-8 d.)

14. Instruct them to "hold up" on a batted ball
     hit into the air.

     The experiences you'll have relating to the
     fly ball rule will test your character as a
     coach. Without belaboring it further,

T-8 c.   Get a good piece of the bag
          while running the bases.

T-8 d.   Runners face the infield, right foot
          forward, knowing where the ball is.

practice drills on this subject are essential. Make the drills realistic. Have infielders, runners on base, and have the coach hit fly balls and ground balls and see what the base runners do.

And be prepared to be patient.

15.   Teach the base runner at second, when no force play is possible, to be cautious about running when the ball is hit in front of him. The runner may not be tuned-in to the third base coach, so he must be taught not to aid the defense by running into a tag at shortstop when he doesn't have to.

16.   Coach them to be aware of base runners ahead of them.

This is especially important with your best players, because they will be the fast, aggressive runners who will forget about Wilber just ahead of them who is unwittingly transfixed on the base paths.

17.   And lastly, the sliding game is really a game for advanced players. Nothing can turn a kid against baseball quicker than a scraped knee, or other injury. Bigger players need to slide for advantage and safety. Little ones don't.

You don't have sufficient time to teach sliding and you probably don't have the proper facilities. Learning to slide on a hard dirt infield, or even in the outfield grass, is not the place to learn for these little guys. A sand pit is more like it. But save it for latter...for the older boys. You've have plenty of other things to teach them.

USE THIS SPACE FOR YOUR NOTES

T - 9   ORGANIZING PRACTICES

Most teeball coaches are hard working dads who have
very little time to schedule practices. Unfortunately,
for a coach to really know how to run his team, to
know which players are doing well at what positions,
to know which players are hitting, to know how to
achieve the most efficient batting order, and to
teach the kids to perform at a reasonably efficient
level (relatively speaking) the coach must schedule
and attend numerous practices himself.

But there's no time for that.

Luckily, the opposing coaches do not have enough time
either. You'll find a few firemen, or successful
sole proprietors able to schedule more practices than
the rest, but that will be the exception, and there's
no real proof that that little extra time they have
is really producing better teams for them.

In fact, children at this age don't have the interest
nor dedication to make numerous practices beneficial.
Some may even get "turned off" to baseball, and
disinterested if they are forced into an excessive
practice routine, not to mention what it does to the
working parents who find it difficult transporting
their children to and from practices.

So the restrictions on Dad's time, and the inadvis-
ability of scheduling numerous practices dictate that
he get the most out of each practice. This requires,
therefore, preparedness, organization, full participation and attendance by the players, and the help of

assistant coaches and parents.

But we don't want to give children of this age group
the impression we're running a military school all
complete with a high level of scheduling, regimenta-
tion and efficiency. We have to remember that it's a
game we're involved in. We want the kids to enjoy
the sport; have fun at it, and as a result look
forward to it. We also want to accomplish a high
level of attendance at practice. If they dread it,
your attendance will diminish drastically and you
won't be able to trade them, fine them or reduce
their salaries.

I think a somewhat "low-key" but highly organized
approach to practice is the best. Schedule no more
than two practices a week, each lasting from 60 to 90
minutes. The 90 minute practice is preferable because
it conditions them for the amount of time they may
spend on the field in a regular game, and it gives
you time to do more things with them. An hours
practice, especially when considering late arrivals,
is pretty short.

In preparing for the first game, however, it's beneficial to schedule three or four practices a week
(for a two or three week period).

During the regular part of the season when one and
two practices a week are conducted, you can place
some of the responsibility for improving on the
parents by giving the players homework. Dad and
mom can help; so can big brother. Playing catch
with the teeballer; fielding their hitting; and
even bringing them to a ball game can all act as
instructional practice. However, their dads should
not force them to sit in front of the T.V. for
extended lengths of time "learning" the game. They
are still too young for that.

Teeballers do need to get in shape, but their general
fitness cannot be changed by what you want to do with
them twice a week. Fortunately their little bodies
have been running around crazy in the neighborhood
and school every day so it is not as if they were
geriatric cases. However, they do have certain
muscles that can be strengthened for throwing,
hitting and running. So by having them do as much of
that as practicable will strengthen those muscles and
improve their performance.

You will notice, however, that at times some of the
children will appear to be out-of-shape. They will
seem weak and their endurance will seem low during
some practices. But just wait until that practice
ends, and you may find them running around crazy
again throwing their gloves at each other with an
abundance of energy, and endurance. Where did all
the energy come from all of a sudden? Their tired-
ness, I would venture to guess, was a result of
boredom and stress rather than lack of energy. That
is another reason why it's important to make
practices fun, and active.

During the seasons I coached teeball I usually
conducted two or three practices a week before the
opening game, and then once a week each for an hour
and a half thereafter. If you don't feel your team
is going to be competitive without more practice,
then you have the right and duty to schedule more
practices. Few things are worse on a child's appreciation of the game than to be on a team that loses
all its games. It is demoralizing, ungratifying,
unhealthy, and should be avoided.

I would also recommend holding your weekly practice
as late in the week as possible; Thursday afternoon
or evening is fine. Believe it or not, the children
seem to perform better during Saturday's game when
their last practice was held within the past two
days.

Here are some other guidelines, then, for conducting
efficient and productive practices:

Practice Guidelines

1. In your introductory practice invite the
   parents to attend. In starting practice
   gather the parents and children in a group,
   and ask the parents to stand behind their
   respective children.

   And commence introductions. First start by
   introducing yourself and your assistant
   coach. Tell them a little about your
   coaching philosophy, and experience, and
   then proceed to introduce your child for
   the benefit of his teammates. Emphasize
   that you expect your players to know each
   others names because it could be important
   in a game situation.

Then proceed to have your assistant coach introduce himself and his child (player), and then have the parents introduce themselves and their respective children (players). Ask for addresses and phone numbers of every player if you didn't get them already.

Then welcome the fathers to help coach, and ask them to approach you for their specific assignments. Make a list of their names and availability. They may be able to help you in a pinch.

If you didn't ask for team mother(s) in your first phone calls to the parents, do it now. The team mother(s) can take a big organi-zational load off your back if they are organized and are willing to do a little work. Two team mothers is better than one from their standpoint as well as yours.

Inform the parents about your anticipated practice schedule, team pictures, and what you know about the league, and game schedule or anything else that comes to mind that they should know about.

Unlike baseball for grown kids or adults, parents of five to eight year-olds usually have a considerable degree of concern about their childrens sports activity. And they should. They have a right to know whether their child's coach is a nice, moral guy, and if he is capable of teaching their child the right things about teeball. So comfort them by showing them that you're not a victory monger, and that you are very interested in their child's well-being, development, interest and enjoyment of the game.

2.   At the first practice of the season intro-
duce your players to a teeball, glove, bat, and tee. Show them how they are used. Tell them about baseball shoes. Ask them questions, and get their responses to see if they know what these articles are. Find out if they have ever used them; if they

play catch with their dads or brothers; why they want to play teeball, and all those kinds of things. Get to know them to find out where they are starting from, so you'll know what to teach them, and so you'll be gratified at the end of the year that you were able to teach them as much as you did.

Then tell them you want to see how well they can throw and catch. Have them form two lines throwing distance apart (which will be about 10 feet). For those needing a lot of help, and there will be a few, ask the fathers to play catch with them at that distance. It doesn't help a child learn how to catch if the kid throwing the ball to him never throws it properly.

Observe how they throw and catch, and make notes on the exceptional ones, good or bad. This will tell you at what level you will have to design practices, and it may give you a quick insight as to what players to think about using at your key "out" positions.

Watch their throwing accuracy and strength. Notice their fielding ability on ground balls and short fly balls.

When you find some obvious trait that some or all are doing wrong, call "time-out" and demonstrate how it should be done correctly.

And then have them continue playing catch to see if any have learned from your demonstration.

In total, have them throw for 15 to 20 minutes, and then change the subject. Their little minds are not accustomed to a concentrated effort on one or two related subjects for a long period of time.

Next have them do some running for you.

Have them run 60 foot races using your assistant coach and a parent or two as the starting and finishing lines. Again, it may help if you make some short notes on the exceptional ones, both fast and slow.

15 minutes of that should be enough; It's now time to have them do a little batting for you. While two or three are preparing to bat, and the other three or four are in their fielding positions, any leftovers should play catch again with any helpers. (It's important to keep the kids busy, and to fully utilize the time you have. If the kids are standing around doing nothing, it's hurting them more than helping them.)

Once everybody has had a turn at bat, and you have at least made some mental notes on who hits well and who doesn't, and what some of their batting problems are, call them into a group and show them how to bat properly.

Many of your players will learn more quickly from other players than they will from the coach. So if you can identify two or three leaders that have nearly the proper form, use them as examples.

3.   Plan your practices in advance. If you're conducting 90 minute practices, it's probably best to change subjects every 15 to 20 minutes so the children won't get easily bored and unattentive. That means you'll have to plan ahead to conduct four or five different functions in your practice schedule.

The five major functions would be:

    a. playing catch

    b. hitting off the tee

    c. base running

    d. fielding off the bat

    e. fielding with base runners

Subcategories of the above would then give you the variation needed to keep their attention.

a. playing catch
    (1) playing catch with a teammate
    (2) playing catch with a coach
    (3) short distance
    (4) longer distance
    (5) ground balls
    (6) short fly balls

b. hitting off the tee
    (1) hitting anywhere
    (2) hitting at home plate
    (3) directional hitting
    (4) hitting and running

c. base running
    (1) running off the bat
    (2) running drills to first base
    (3) drills to other bases from a
        stop
    (4) drills to other bases from
        batting
    (5) the fly ball drill
    (6) the run-down drill
    (7) stopping on the bag
    (8) listening for the base coach

d. fielding off the bat
    (1) fielding ground balls
    (2) fly balls
    (3) fielding and throwing to
        first
    (4) throwing to other bases
    (5) tagging the runner
    (6) practicing the run-down
    (7) practicing at different
        positions
    (8) drills related
        to the pitching circle
    (9) covering home
   (10) backing-up in the outfield

e. defensive fielding with base
   runners
    (1) getting the out at first
    (2) getting the force-out at
        other bases
    (3) getting the out at home plate
    (4) outfield throws to the proper
        base
    (5) backing-up the outfield
        throws

(6) bases loaded situations
(7) holding the runner at third
(8) double play off a fly out
(9) and many others

I always started my teeball practices with
"playing catch". It is essential to start
with "catch" so that their arms get properly warm for other activities, and because
the late arrivals won't miss some coaching
technicalities that aren't covered more
than once.

Besides, the kids seem to like playing
catch the least. Some are afraid of the
ball, but most can't do the things with a
baseball that make it interesting, like
being able to catch. It turns into hard
work for them just to get out there and
play catch. So we get that out of the way
first.

I would like to recommend that since they
have to learn how to catch from each others
throws that that is where practice starts.
Have them form two lines and have them play
catch with each other; good players with
good players, and poorer players with poorer
players. But they will all need a lot of
supervision here as their two lines will
quickly disintegrate, and balls will be
flying every-which-way. Kids who are afraid
of the ball, and lack catching skills will
start 15 feet from their partner and end up
as far away from them as possible reducing
their catching challenge to picking up a
slow grounder that's about ready to stop
rolling.

Batting practice, however, is like dessert
to them, so I always left batting last. I
would even use it occasionally to entice
them into greater diligence at some of the
other practice subjects. For example, if
someone was really cutting-up, I might
threaten with not letting him take batting
practice. Now that I look back, I don't
think I ever had to enforce that threat.

You may decide that some of the kids need

special work in a given area, and it is
beneficial if you take those aside and work
with them on those problems while the other
coach or parents help conduct drills with
the rest of the kids. Kids who are hitting
the ball well may need more base running
practice than those who cannot hit the ball
at all.

4.   Keep your players busy at practice.

Whatever time you dedicate to practice each
week, make sure you don't have players
wasting time doing nothing. It won't be
easy for you to keep them busy. Young
children need a lot of supervision to keep
their time productive. You'll need the
help of your assistant coach and perhaps a
parent or two.

You will quickly discover that conducting a
teeball practice is nothing like conducting
one with more mature players. With more
mature players you can set up a practice
function (playing catch for example), and
come back ten minutes later and your team
will still be playing catch. When you set
up teeballers in a practice function, you
can blow your nose and look up over the top
of your handkerchief to discover they are
doing everything except what you just set
them up to do. Some kids are chasing the
balls into the bushes; some are throwing
their gloves at each other; and others are
just laying down because they are tired.

Nonetheless, your job is to get as much
coaching and practice into the allotted
time as possible, and if you allow kids to
stand idle, it's a real shame. Even during
batting practice when you need a few
fielders to stand in the field to shag
balls, if a batter comes up that can't or
never hits to left field, go out a play
catch with the left fielder; throw him
some ground balls, or teach him how to
back-up, or move at the swing of the bat.
If a weak player is just hitting nubbers
back to the pitcher, don't just let the
rest of the field stand there, that does not

do them any good. In fact it does them a
lot of harm. They get bored and disinterested. Hit them ground balls or something.

I can't emphasize enough the importance of
having fully packed, busy practices. It
would be a grievous mistake to have the
parents take time to bring Johnny to practice, and Johnny take 90 minutes of his
time to throw and catch the ball 10 times,
hit the ball 5 times and stand idle for the
rest of practice waiting for something to
happen. That amount of activity he could
have been done at home in five minutes.
That is another reason why playing catch is
so vital to the practice forum, because in
a very short time each child can experience
a high volume of activity; 30-40-50 throws
and almost as many attempts at catches.

5.   Make sure you enlist the parents' help.

If any parents are standing around at practice who are not watching other siblings,
invite them to help. Even if it's just
playing catch with an idle outfielder.
They will give you immense help in keeping
the children productive, and the parents
will enjoy getting involved with you, and
probably gain some appreciation on how
tough your job really is.

The ideal situation would be to have a coach
for every child. But you can settle for and
achieve considerable with your assistant coach
and two or three parent helpers. You may find
them quietly observing practice from a
distance. Just go over to them and invite them
to help out by mentioning something specific
like, "How about playing catch with little Joe
in the outfield?", or "Would you mind being
umpire?", or "Could you coach third base for
us?".

Obviously, you'll have to stay in charge
of all this help. But you should think of
your-self more as the "chief coordinator"
rather than the "supreme head coach". A
"supreme head coach" has full authority,
and power. But you're a volunteer-amateur.

You won't receive the same reverence as a full-time paid coach, and some dad's may try to move into your responsibility zone. Don't overreact, they are just honestly interested in their child's well-being. Listen to their ideas. State your preference, and ask them to help do it your way. Be "a-matter-of-fact" with them.

6. When you set up the practice schedule, try to set consistent times, days, and locations so that your schedule has a chance of becoming a habit with the kids and parents.

   You will be rewarded by having better attendance at practice, and it will save your team mothers and yourself from having to make numerous phone calls informing the players or parents of the next practice time and location. By the way, telling the children the details of the next practice, just won't make it. They'll forget, get confused, pick the wrong time, day, place, and your team will suffer the consequences.

7. Try to locate and use a practice field that has most of the same characteristics that you'll experience at the games.

   If the ball diamond at the games is made of dirt, find a dirt infield somewhere to practice on. If the parks are out of diamonds, look for one at the local school or church. The more the children practice on a field similar to the one they will play their game on, the more comfortable, and less distracted they will feel during the game.

   Try to practice as often as possible with real base bags or a close facsimile. Imaginary bags such a baseball glove, or any other target will suffice if no real bags are available, but with real bags anchored to the ground the kids can get a better feel for turning to the next base, or stopping on the bag.

8. Make sure you have the proper equipment for the children to practice with.

The minimum practice equipment should consist of:

    a. one teeball for every two players

    b. three lightweight bats, preferably of different sizes and weights

    c. one tee

    d. one fairly decent base

Additional desirable equipment would be:

    a. a few extra teeballs because the children manage to lose some during practices and games

    b. two or three extra bats of different sizes and weights because a child needs a choice as to which of the bats feels comfortable to him

    c. one or two extra tees because batting practice can be given to two or three at a time with the help of a couple of assistants

    d. an extra glove because children frequently misplace their own

    e. a first-aid kit because Timmy's dad may have taught him how to slide

I would also recommend that the coach bring a few things of his own to practice with. Unless you're a "gentleman coach" you'll need baseball shoes, a glove, a whistle, a clipboard, your practice plan notes, the team roster with the names of the parents, and occasionally a stopwatch.

Since it will be very important for you to demonstrate how things should be done including running, I would advise wearing the appropriate attire for exercise. Sometimes, to get into the spirit of the thing, I would wear part of my slow-pitch baseball uniform; stirrups, baseball pants, sweatshirt and cap. It helped me get into the proper mood to coach, and it may have even set a better atmosphere for the children.

9. Develop an opening and closing practice routine.

    Gather the kids together for a couple of minutes at both ends of the practice to prepare them for what you are about to do, or review what you just have done.

    Give the assistant coach a chance to contribute some of the things he feels should be said.

10. Make sure you have some type of beverage at practice especially when the park does not have a drinking fountain.

11. Do not leave any of the children at the park after practice. If their parents are late picking them up, stay with them, bring them home, or have a standing rule that the child can be retrieved at your house.

Now that you have everything organized for practice,
your job of teaching and drilling the physical fundamentals is going to be much easier. You feel
confident about your plan, and what you need to
instruct. And so you proceed to tackle the numerous
elements of the physical fundamentals one by one
keeping in mind that no matter how good you are the
children are limited to how much they will learn in
such a short period of time. They do not need to
learn everything right away, and you are prepared to
allow for a large margin of error at this level of
baseball. In other words, you're organized, disci-
plined, regimented, knowledgeable and motivated, but
your expectations are under control, and you're going
to keep cool about it.

1.   Throwing. (Review chapter T - 5.)

       You'll have to give them an example of the
       proper way to throw a teeball. If you
       haven't played much baseball, and are not
       confident that you can show them properly,
       no problem; just find some young high-
       schooler, or neighbor, or whomever throws
       pretty well, and ask him to demonstrate to
       the children how to throw. Make sure the
       demonstration follows the principles out-
       lined in chapter T-5, and you can't miss.

Play catch with another adult in front of
the children so they can see how easy it
is, and how it should be done. Maybe they
have never seen someone play catch before.
Don't throw the ball too hard, because it
could frighten them. Nice and easy tosses.
Twenty or thirty of them, and make sure
they're watching.

Show them a few easy underhand tosses too.
Some of the children may not be able to
start with balls tossed at them in the air,
and picking up a rolling underhand toss
could be a good starting point.

If you're at the <u>flyweight</u> level the
next step will be to have them form a
single line with coaching staff and helpers
forming a parallel line ten feet away.
Make sure everyone is spread out sufficiently to allow for inaccurate throws.
Now the children can start throwing to
their targets for 10 to 15 minutes. If
you're able to get free from playing catch,
you should wander around observing the
throwing idiosyncrasies of each childs
throw and correcting strong fundamental
errors. If many have the same problem,
call "time-out" and demonstrate what most
are doing wrong and how it should be done
properly.

The <u>mightymite</u> level may be advanced
enough where some of the kids can play
catch with each other. But keep their
distances uniform and under control. Even
mightymiters will tend to spread out on you
for various reasons, and you need them
fairly close together so that a lot of
throws and catches can be accomplished in
a reasonably short period of time.

Have them throw at different distances, and
keep track who has the strong arms. It's
best to start at a short distance with many
throws, then progress to greater distances,
say 40 feet, but never over 60 feet. The
shorter distances build confidence and
allow for a higher quantity of throws in a
short period of time.

When you have selected fielding positions, some part of your throwing practice should be from their fielding position to the pitcher or base they would most likely be throwing to in a game.

2.   Catching.   (Review chapter T - 6.)

Once the children have put their gloves on properly, and patted them into shape and flexibility, it's best to demonstrate with an assistant on how a ball should be caught. Have the thrower move the ball around on you as you show them the different positions of the glove in catching balls thrown to a variety of locations within reach of your glove.

Not too many <u>flyweighters</u> will be able to catch at all, so when they are lined up to play catch with an adult, the distance should be very close between thrower and catcher, and the ball should be delivered to the child with an underhand lob. Once you find out who can catch, and a few might be able to catch a little, you can have them play catch together.

You will find many more <u>mightymiters</u> able to catch, but still at the low end of the efficiency scale. It would still be pre-ferable to use an assistant as their throw-ing partner so that the balls are delivered in a uniform manner, and usually within reach of their glove.

The main problem with having the players play catch with each other is that many cannot throw or catch well enough to keep the ball going back and forth in an effi-cient manner. The children have to get in as many throws and catches as possible in the short period of time alloted, and most of the time playing catch with each other can be very inefficient.

Once you have seen them play catch for awhile it's time to show them the "glove position drill". They form a line across the top of the letter "t", and you position yourself at the bottom of the "t" with your back to them. An assistant facing you with a ball in his hand places the ball high, low, wide and at you, and you demonstrate the proper way to position your glove in catching balls thrown to those positions. The children behind you should them emulate what you're doing, so they get used to turning their gloves the right way on balls to the left, right, high and low. (See the examples in figures T-10 a, and T-10 b.)

Then have the children form two lines facing each other, and perform the same drill with the other child providing the held direction of the ball. Correct those who are reaching for the ball improperly. Tell them it's like picking christmas bulbs off the tree. If you see a child having a difficult time with this, give him some special time on a one-on-one basis. This drill can do a lot in improving a childs catching ability.

The best drill for learning how to catch is no secret to baseball players. And that's just playing catch. The more of it they do, regardless how inefficient they are doing it, the more they will improve. It's much better than infield practice, because there is a greater quantity of throws and catches in the same amount of time. And spend a lot of time on it.

Conducting drills on fielding ground balls can easily be combined with playing catch, but I don't think it's a good idea to necessarily mix them together from throw to throw. A ground ball is the most unpre-dictable thing the children will have to deal with in teeball save a thrown bat. Since ground balls can frighten them and hurt their fielding confidence, ground ball practice should be conducted under close and isolated conditions. They need to know that the speed of the ball is going to be consistent, and especially on grass, the balls should be tossed with a high level of delicacy.

T-10 a.   See if the fielder reaches
            for the ball the proper way.

T-10 b.   Move it around on him slowly, then
            faster.   Left, right, up, down.

Underhand tosses are initially the best way
to begin learning how to field ground
balls. Grass is fine for a while, but some
infield (dirt) practice is essential. If
no dirt infield is available for practices,
outside basketball courts will do. But
remember rubber coated balls on pavement
can do some horrendously tricky things, so
watch the backspin, curvespin, etc.

Ground balls don't have to be batted to
give the children good practice, but balls
hit off the bat do have a different speed
and psychological factor. So give them some
ground balls off the bat too for a well
rounded education. At this level of
competency the children will not be able to
perform a good drill of "pepper." Pepper,
as you may already know, is a practice
routine which has fielders placed at close
range with a batter (say 15 to 20 feet)
serve up easy strikes to the batter to be
hit back to these fielders on the ground
for fielding practice.

As a drill conduct infield practice, or
have them gather in groups of four with
two in front and two to backup, spread out,
and hit easy ground balls to the front two.
Test their range and ability to come up
throwing quickly.

When their skills have improved a little
try throwing or hitting fly balls to them.
The fly balls don't have to be hit too high
into the air for obvious reasons. But nice
and easy pop-ups and fly balls will be fun
for most and good practice.

3.   Hitting.   (Review chapter T - 7.)

Batting practice can take place at the plate
or in a drill format with two or three tees
going simultaneously. During most of the
practices it is more effective to have at
least two tees be used at a time so that
the children can get in as much batting as
possible. And fortunately they don't hit
the ball with such great power as to
require a lot of playground space to bat.

One very effective way to conduct a batting drill is to have three tees spread sufficiently apart facing the foul fence. And have the kids swing away with the teeballs hitting them at the coach backed-up by the fence.

Have them bat enough (30 swings) to get their muscles warm, but when they start getting sloppy and not hitting the ball properly be aware that they may be tiring. A bat is heavy to most of them, and tired swinging can produce some bad habits.

4.   Running the bases.   (Review chapter T - 8.)

The best base running practice of all is to setup actual game situations with infielders, a batter and base runners and let the kids experience life-like predicaments. As they error in their base running choices, stop practice momentarily to show all the players what the base runners should have done. But be as positive as possible...not too critical.

Repetitive drills, of course, can be conducted from any base, and the best place to start is at home plate.

A repetitive drill is one that through the repetition of one or two primary acts forces the athlete into the habit of performing those acts in a similar situation.

Thus, by setting up a drill where the batter swings the bat and immediately batter takes off running to first base can instill this act as a habit perhaps helping him to overcome watching the ball after he has hit it.

The base running drills, then, should all be setup with the players forming a line and taking a turn at performing and repeating one or two primary acts until some desired habitual reaction to the situation arises.

The first drill, for example, can be lining

up and each taking a turn at swinging the
bat at an imaginary ball, and then immediately running to first base. This can be
done five to ten times for each player,
until most understand the concept, and are
doing it automatically.

Running to first and following the first
base coach's running signals can be the
second phase of that drill, and so on.

On another day have the kids all lineup at
first base and run drills relating to first
base and advancing to second and third.

Continue around the bases all the way
through home plate, and then recall the
drills frequently throughout the year.
Concentrate on important problem areas in
terms of their proper priority. For
example, if the kids are not getting to
first frequently because of something they
are doing in running to first, then don't
spend much time with them in a drill
scoring from third.

The base running drills can be one of the
most productive, and fun exercises you are
involved in as a coach. Kids love to run
wild, and play games. You can setup the
situations to be challenging, rewarding and
fun for them, and you will enjoy it quite-
a-bit yourself.

5.   Infield practice.

Infield practice is essential in teaching
the children the real essence of the game
of baseball.

Once you have selected your infield, you
will probably have decided that the ones
playing the outfield have little fielding
skills, and need some maturing and growth
before they will improve much. So you've
got to concentrate on giving the infielders
as much practice as possible so the game
can be conducted in some semblance of
order. The outfielders, therefore, must
act as the base runners, or backup the

infielding plays. This will be a way to
keep the outfielders active, and you should
see their base running and outfielding
skills improve considerably.

I guess what I'm really trying to say is that
you can't feel guilty about giving some
selected children more practice of a certain
type that the others especially when the
maturity factor is involved. In most team
sports the second unit is crucial in helping
give the first unit the "prime cut" of practice
when graduation occurs and the second unit,
presumably comprised of the younger kids
will move up to the strategic positions and
then they will get the "prime cut" of
practice.

Of course, you can't overdo it either. Be
observant of when the runners are getting
tired and even when the infielders need to
do a little running. Rotate the functions
with discretion, but give greater concentration of practice to the key positions.
Your limited practice time dictates this
requirement.

Fielding drills, in general, should be
designed to place the fielders in an environment that most resembles the game situation. At first you can proceed with imaginary runners, and then add real runners.
Runners provide many things to the environment you're trying to create, but the most
important thing they contribute is the
timing criteria for achieving an "out".

You need to set up the game situations you
feel need practicing. Bat the ball yourself to assure the ball goes where you want
it to go. Set up base runners artificially
at the bases you need occupied if getting
them there in the normal progression is not
successful.

Start with the most common situations such
as plays on the batter at first, and then
progress around the bases eventually mixing
in pop flies, force-outs, and run-downs.

Develop some backup players for all your

infield positions. You're sure to have
some children come down with a cold to two,
and a little bit of practice at these
positions for the backup player can go
along way in preparing him for that
position.

During the fielding drills, stop the action
as a teacher would and point out things
they should be doing and things they
shouldn't. Address the coaching to all the
players, not just the one whose act you're
trying to correct.

Use what works for your own unique person-
ality, but by all means be demonstrative.
I used to kid with them and even make fun
of them in trying to get a point across at
times. Sometimes I even showed them a
little anger, especially when they were
goofing off, or not paying attention. I
would frequently ask them if they had
wanted to join a baseball team or circus.
And I spread the criticisms around
pretty evenly. One must be careful not to
criticize one position too frequently, and
always counter it with frequent praises,
and accolades.

And the most important thing regarding
fundamentals; don't let them do things in
practice that you wouldn't want them to do
in the game. They should throw in practice
as you would want them to throw in the
game, and they should field in practice as
you would want them to field in the game.

6.   The safety rules.

Review the safety rules of teeball with
them frequently especially when you see
them doing things that may be dangerous.

Some of these rules are:
      a.   Always look where you are throw-
            ing the ball.

      b.   Never stand near someone who is
            swinging a bat.

c.   Only swing a bat in designated
     areas, at designated times.

d.   Look around before you swing a
     bat to make sure nobody will get
     hit.

e.   Do not throw your gloves into the
     air.

f.   Do not throw rocks or other things.

g.   Do not slide.

USE THIS SPACE FOR YOUR NOTES

Once the Parks Department or any other organization that may be sponsoring the Teeball League has selected the players that are to comprise your team, and once you have been given the roster and receive the schedule (the schedule usually comes later than the roster), the organization, and administration of the team is completely up to you.

You are the one that will have to make the initial contact with the players' parents, and the players themselves. From there you'll have to plan, organize, coordinate and administer all the functions required of a successful organization. If you plan it right, with a little luck, a good assistant coach and team mothers, your work load will be light, enjoyable, successful and quite rewarding.

Here's a list of some of the things you should consider:

1.   The level of shared responsibilities and authority with the assistant coach.

      Hopefully, you will have an amiable, supportive, and efficient assistant coach. It is preferable to have one that is technically competent; one who wants to influence your coaching and strategy, rather than wrestle from you the leadership of the team. You volunteered to be the head

coach and assume the responsibilities of its
success and failure, and unless you deserve a
mutiny you can expect him to be supportive.
By the way, losing is not a justification for
mutiny.

It will be important for you to assess the level
of involvement you will need from your assistant
coach and the level of involvement he expects.
Communicate this up front so you'll both avoid
problems and be able to take advantage of each
others strengths and availability.

2.   The recruiting of team mothers, and the assign-
     ment of their responsibilities.

A team mother can be more than one person and
contrary to popular belief, they neither have to
be female nor mothers. I will have to admit,
however, that I have never had a dad volunteer
to be team mother.

Some of their most important responsibilities
could be:

   a.   making phone calls to the parents to keep
        them informed of the practice schedule,
        team pictures, games, locations and any
        other team events.

   b.   organizing the parents in bringing the
        beverages and after game refreshments for
        the players.

   c.   helping with any player transportation
        problems that arise.

   d.   coordinating the team picture function
        including the collection of money if
        necessary.

   e.   helping the players maintain the proper
        batting order during the game while the two
        coaches are coaching the bases.

   f.   doing things that have to do with the team
        uniform such as picking up the team uniform,
        passing them out to the parents, getting
        names on the jerseys (if desired), and
        picking up pants, socks or other things

that may not initially come with the uniform supplied by the Parks Department.

g. doing whatever else, administratively
    speaking, may be helpful to the coaches
    such as organ-izing team outings, picnics
    and year end awards.

There is no doubt about it, the recruiting of
good team mothers may be the most important
thing you do as a coach. They can do a lot to
share the work load, enhance team morale through
good communications with the parents, and pave
the way for a happy, family oriented team effort.

3. Recruiting and instructing the team official
    scorer.

The scoring in teeball differs significantly
from the scoring in advanced baseball. The main
purpose of scoring in teeball is to assure the
original batting lineup is preserved, and the
total score is accurate.

Both teams have a scorer. They normally check
with the umpire at the end of each teams "at
bat" to assure that the accumulation of runs is
accurate. The umpire will frequently rely on
the scorers in helping him sort out the details
of the last play.

In advanced baseball the scorer can record all
types of statistical information to help the
team strategists use the law-of-averages to its
full advantage. Most of this is unnecessary in
teeball, and not too practical to attempt to
accumulate. On the other hand the more information you have on your players and the opponents,
the better you are able to review performances
and make the proper adjustments toward the
improvement of the team.

The league will normally hand out scorebooks
with the equipment or uniforms, but they can be
purchased inexpensively at most sports shops.
Instructions on how to score the game are in-
cluded with most scorebooks, so that won't be
covered here, but I will include recommendations
on what will be necessary for you to keep track

of in teeball and what isn't necessary.

Keep track of:

a. Children maintaining their proper batting order.

b. The advancement of each child on the bases.

c. Outs.

d. The scoring of each base runner, preferably by filling in the diamond on the scorebook so it stands out.

e. The direction and distance of batted balls. This is done merely by drawing a line on the diagram of the field of play on the scorebook to show where the ball was hit. An arching line can indicate a fly ball. A solid straight line indicates a hard hit fly ball or line drive. And a hard hit ground ball can be shown as a line with several dips in it.

Keeping track of very poorly hit balls is important too, so that the pitcher call be warned, for example, that the batter will probably hit the ball just in front of the plate, and that he should be ready to field the ball there.

Don't keep track of:

a. Strikes.

b. The difference between a hit and an error.

c. Runs batted in.

Lastly, your official scorer should be one who will arrive to the game early to help you record your official lineup and present the lineup to the umpire. This person should also be vocal during the game to keep you informed of batting order infractions, or other problems as soon as they occur.

On offense, the scorer can sit at the end of the bench and "clear" each batter in accordance with the batting order.

On defense, the scorer can let you know where the batter has been hitting the ball, and toward the middle of the order, how many batters are left.

4. Decide on team uniform accessories.

Your league may just issue certain parts of the uniform such as a cap and a shirt. Some parents will want you to have full uniforms which means collecting money for pants, belt, stirrups, undersocks, and perhaps a color coordinated undershirt.

Those little people can get pretty excited about having a full uniform and they can look pretty cute too. But the hazard in requiring uniformity is that some parents just may not be able to afford spending $15-25 more on uniform accessories when it really isn't necessary.

To hurdle such a decision, may I suggest you have the team mothers take a quick census of the parents to discover how much the full outfit is desired. If there are one or two that don't want it because of financial considerations, perhaps some disguised funding can be done so that all the players match.

Other accessories may include the following:
- iron-on player names
- additional iron-on numbers
- special emblems for the caps
- special iron-on ornamentations like stars

Some parents like to decorate their kid's shirts and caps with all kinds of "cute" slogans, names and things, such as, "The Kid", "Big Tom", "No. 1". Discourage this because baseball is a team concept which demands a certain amount of uniformity. Special slogans belong on stock cars not team uniforms.

With all the potential for disharmony, the coach can do much to avoid problems by deciding, establishing and communicating the way it's to be

from the beginning. Having flexibility for
things that are not that important, and firmness
on the things that are. The parents will go
along with the coach, especially when he takes a
position before they even thought of the
question.

Strive for uniformity, whether with or without
full uniforms and accessories. There could be
damage to the "team" concept if a few players
are decked out in full garb while others arrive
in a shirt and holey blue jeans.

5.   Incentives and rewards.

The coach should consider providing the children
with incentives, and rewards. This may help
promote the level of concentration, and help the
children feel good about themselves even if they
are a team that is not winning.

The coach can use iron-on stars as the incentive.
He can purchase a box or two and inform the kids
that they will earn these stars to be put on
their jerseys for outstand-ing performances in a
game. The presentation of the stars can be made
every three or four games, based on a very
liberal set of criteria. Some kids can earn
four stars for four games, but all should earn at
least one star.

Positive reinforcement should be used in the
star awards. A child who earns one star must be
praised, as well as the child who has earned
four.

I awarded stars quite liberally every three or
four games instead of every game so that I
wouldn't be pinned down as to exactly which game
the child was receiving a star. By the end of
the season the best players had the most stars,
but even the worst players had three or four
stars they could be proud of.

I presented the stars in envelopes with a short
photocopied note telling each player how important his contribution was to the team. The note
also reminded them on what part of the uniform
they were to affix the stars. The right sleeve
was used for outstanding performance stars, and

the left sleeve was used for team captain stars.
You may prefer to have the stars affixed to the
baseball caps. Every child was team captain at
least once even if he shared it with another
player as co-captain. Some were captain more
than once. .

6.   You'll have to develop rules as to player
     conduct.

     Tardiness to practice and the games, and misbe-
     havior are the two most frequent disciplinary
     problems.

     Be firm, but not too harsh. Although you need
     to maintain a certain level of timliness and
     orderliness, don't be so strict with a child as
     to jeopardize his future in sports to satisfy
     this requirement. It is better to sacrifice the
     team rather than the player at this stage of
     baseball.

     By the way, on windy days orderliness may be
     more than difficult. Something just happens to
     the kids that makes them hyperactive. Now this
     may be more prevalent in dry arid climates than
     humid tropical climates, but just be aware of
     it. When it happens, try to set up games that
     can corral their hyperactivity into something
     productive. Enjoy it. Don't over discipline
     it.

7.   You'll have to help the league in enforcing
     rules concerning parent conduct.

     I never had a problem in this category and I do
     think the problem is infrequent. But be pre-
     pared anyway to inform a rowdy parent that the
     league has certain rules governing foul language,
     abuse, agitating umpires, and razzing the
     opposing players.

     This can be communicated to the parents before
     the season starts in a short memo so that all
     are aware of it.

USE THIS SPACE FOR YOUR NOTES

T - 12   THE UMPIRES

Your league will probably extend quite a effort in
obtaining good umpires for the games, but you should
realize right from the beginning that there will be
some inherent problems in trying to have the games
officiated like advanced baseball.

Those factors preventing the best officiating may be:

a. that there is little or no pay to attract
   good umpires.

b. that the league can financially support, and
   can only find one umpire to work each game.

c. that there aren't experienced umpires in the
   area.

d. that potential umpires may not make a successful transition from advanced baseball
   rules to teeball rules.

e. that the umpires selected as a group have no
   formal league association and may be inconsistent from umpire to umpire.

f. that the game of teeball itself, since played
   at a very low level of performance in relationship to the rules, creates many more
   umpire involvement decisions that increase
   the chance of a bad call.

g. that the teeball rules surrounding the pitching circle and the midway base runners line, however necessary to the game, invite controversy.

You will probably find that most of the umpires officiating your games are young people interested in learning to umpire as a part-time job. They may, in fact, be officiating the game for the first time, and may be nervous, unsure of the application of some of the rules, easily intimidated, and positioned to have a bad day.

This, obviously, can be very disconcerting to an experienced teeball coach like yourself, but it can end up being no problem at all if you step back and remember to put the game in its proper perspective. The quality control for all the elements of teeball are rather consistent with each other, and that includes player ability, coaching ability, umpiring ability, and the importance of the game.

One thing you have a right to expect from the umpires is a consistent and unbiased approach in administering the rules. This means that the umpire can show no favoritism. He may inadvertently lack consistency in the application of the rules because of his lack of expertise, but as long as he is equally unfair to both sides in general, you have little room for complaint.

Our league upheld very stringent rules governing the manner in which coaches, players and fans were allowed to interface with the umpires. I support those rules wholeheartedly. It really isn't good for the children to see someone abusing the umpires. The children begin to believe it's an acceptable part of the game, and to some extent their focus on the results of their own performance begins to diminish as they learn (wrongly so) that the umpires have more influence in the outcome of the game than do the players.

Another problem inherent in the officiating of teeball games is that there is usually only one umpire assigned to the game. This is really not enough to catch all the infractions that go on all the time considering that you will have anywhere from nine to twelve batters come to the plate in an inning, the bases are always full of runners, and there could be

14 fielders out in the field; So we have base runners crossing the plate at the same time tags are
being made at second base; perhaps the pitcher is in
and out of the pitching circle while other base
runners are advancing the bases.

When you take into consideration the magnitude of the
umpire's job, and his level of experience, and the
relative importance of the game, you have a lot of
reasons not to overreact to his erroneous decisions.

However, you can do certain things to try to insure
that you and the umpire have a clear understanding of
what the common rules are covering the important and
often controversial facets of the game.

There were certain rules I always tried to clear-up
at the beginning of the game during the miniconference
that is conducted by the umpire with the opposing
coaches. Those rules were:

   a. a clear definition of the in-play and out-of-
      play area.

   b. the umpires interpretation of when a tipped
      ball was in play (the batting circle).

   c. does the umpire consider it a dead ball when
      the pitcher controls the ball and runs through
      the pitching circle.

   d. on the last play of the side is the base
      runner awarded home if he has passed the
      halfway mark but not reached home if the
      pitcher has possession of the ball in the
      pitching circle with no play being made on
      the runner at first.

The above questions and others you may experience
need clarifying before each game because different
umpires interpret the rules differently.

As the game proceeds and certain strong points of
question arise as to the umpires judgements and
interpretations, you have the right to call "time
out" and discuss the rule interpretation with the
umpire. You do not have a right to debate his judgement, but you do have a right to discuss his interpretation of the rules. In all cases, by the way,
discussions should not be conducted across the infield but in close quarters with the umpire.

The coach has the responsibility to protect his players within the rules. For example: if a ball is hit into the outfield, and the fielder is interfered with by a kid playing in a close-by soccer game, this has got to be brought to the attention of the umpire who may not realize the interference occurred.

Let me repeat that the interference, or any other point of discussion with the umpire should be discussed at close quarters with the umpire in a low key style. Yelling your objection across the field only incites the parents and distracts the children from understanding the most important feature of the game, their own participation, effort and performance.

USE THIS SPACE FOR YOUR NOTES

REORDER FORM

Rush me _____ copies of "Coaching Kids Teeball".

I am enclosing a check or money order to cover the book, @ $6.95 each, plus shipping, handling, and the appropriate state sales tax. See below.

From: (please print)

_____

address:

_____
_____
_____
phone# (   )_____

Qty. ordered _____ @ $6.95 each = $

  plus shipping and handling   +1.50

Subtotal   _____

  local sales tax   +

Total (include ck. with order) $ _____ $

Address the envelope to:

American Youth Sports Publishing Co.
c/o Teeball
24365 San Fernando Road   Suite 193
Newhall, California 91321